mindfulness

A JEWISH APPROACH

MOSAICA PRESS

mindfulness

A JEWISH APPROACH

JONATHAN FEINER, PhD
Foreword by David Pelcovitz, PhD

Published by Mosaica Press, Inc.
www.mosaicapress.com
info@mosaicapress.com

מוסדות אור שמח מרכז טננבאום ע.ר. 58-00-21343-00
רח' שמעון הצדיק 22-28 ירושלים ת.ד. 18103
טל: 02-581-0315

Adar II, 5779

We live in a world of distraction. Overwhelmed with sensory input, digital media, multiple commitments and a cultural milieu that glorifies hedonism, selfishness and ego gratification, we live lives filled with anxiety, tension and indeed silent desperation. This impacts on our service of G-d, the quality of our prayers, the joy or lack thereof in our mitzvot, our relationships to our spouse and our children and ultimately with ourselves. Both *mussar* and *chassidut* emphasize the importance of inner serenity in our Divine service. Rabbi Simcha Zissel Ziv, the Alter of Kelm, remarked, "Take time, be exact, unclutter the mind." Indeed, our Sages taught us long ago that jealousy, lust, and seeking of honor can destroy a person.

Our Torah lays down these values and goals, but many people lack the practical techniques and exercises that can enable and empower them to achieve these goals in their daily lives. Dr. Jonathan Feiner, a gifted therapist deeply committed to helping his patients, has written an incisive and impressive book describing how Torah and mitzvot are not simply formalistic technical rituals but represent a kind of blueprint or template for the fostering of mindfulness, inner peace, disattachment from inappropriate cravings, and relishing the inner joy of the moment instead of dwelling on the past or worrying about the future. Dr. Feiner draws on a wide variety of sources: the teachings of Chazal, the insights of the Baalei Mussar, the inspiration of Chassidus, and the profundities of Kabbalah are deftly joined with contemporary psychology and mindfulness literature to create a comprehensive workable framework to achieve a true inner peace and harmony. This is a book that addresses profoundly important issues, issues with which every sensitive human being must grapple. This work will greatly benefit both the presently noncommitted Jew and the Jew who has been halachically observant for many years. It is my judgment that the tools he is imparting will enhance the spiritual lives of all those who incorporate them.

May the author's efforts be blessed with success.

Yitzchak A. Breitowitz
Rav, Kehillat Ohr Somayach
Jerusalem, Israel

In his seminal work, *Mindfulness: A Jewish Approach*, my esteemed Talmid, Dr. Jonathan Feiner, has pioneered a breakthrough in the field of Jewish Torah Psychology. By developing a system of Torah based mindfulness, Dr. Feiner has given the Jewish psychologist and patient tools with which to achieve complete emotional health using mindfulness in a totally acceptable Torah way. This in itself is a vitally important contribution to our community. But, more than that, the book is a must read for every Torah Jew who can learn an incredible amount of Torah, Musar, and Hashkafa so necessary for spiritual growth in our daily lives and for coping with life's challenges. There are wonderful exercises for us to implement these concepts as well.

I therefore highly recommend this book for all to read, study, and to use as a vital guide to achieve a healthy Torah life.

With blessing for health and Torah,

Rabbi Hershel Reichman
Rosh Yeshiva, RIETS

P: 646.592.4062 F: 646.592.4060 E: riets@yu.edu Web: yu.edu/riets

בס״ד

CONGREGATION KNESETH ISRAEL

728 Empire Avenue   Phone: 718.327.0500   www.whiteshul.org
Far Rockaway, NY 11691   Fax: 718.327.7415   office@whiteshul.com

Rabbi
Rabbi Eytan Feiner

Assistant Rabbi
Rabbi Motti Neuburger

Rabbi Emeritus
Rabbi Ralph Pelcovitz זצ״ל

President
Domenico Antonelli

Executive Vice President
Heshie Lazar

Senior Vice President
Matis Hedvat

Second Vice President
Sadi Benzaquen

**Vice President,
Programming**
Barry Salamon

**Vice President,
Youth**
Yechiel Zlotnick

Secretary
Brian Nadata

Treasurer
Daniel Liss

Legal Counsel
Sidney Lipstein

Chairman of the Board
Chaim Dahan

**Vice Chairmen of
the Board**
*Nesanel Feller
Tuvia Silverstein*

9 Iyar 5779
May 14, 2019

     Weaving together myriad outlooks and insights, illuminating vignettes and life lessons, culled from a vast array of both Jewish and secular sources, Dr. Jonathan Feiner has succeeded beautifully in presenting the reader with a rich and enlightening tapestry on the topic of "mindfulness." Sprinkled with compelling studies and sundry real-life stories, the author's masterful work is written with unusual candor and humility, and he invites us warmly into his own personal journey on the path to attaining true mindfulness.

     Interesting and informative, powerful and thought-provoking, *Mindfulness: A Jewish Approach* challenges us to be more acutely aware and mindful of the present moment, to ponder "the real me," and to pay far closer attention to the people and events that surround us daily. Our gratitude to this brilliant author is immeasurable, and we thank him immensely for his exhaustive research and his generous gift of guiding us through our life's journey to become more genuinely mindful – and better, more profoundly aware, people in the process.

     And I thank the author personally for being a terrific, caring, and selflessly devoted brother throughout our shared journeys – past, present, and future…

With utmost admiration and abundant *nachas*,

Eytan Feiner
Rabbi

Table of Contents

PART I

Foundations

PART II

The Value of Being Present

Foreword

BY DR. DAVID PELCOVITZ

In *Mindfulness: A Jewish Approach*, Dr. Jonathan Feiner does a masterful job educating our minds and hearts in the understanding and practice of Jewish mindfulness. In an age of distraction and fragmentation, this book couples Jewish wisdom with secular approaches in an integrated manner that serves as a roadmap to living life with greater awareness, purpose, and ability to live more fully in the present.

Dr. Feiner has a gift for writing in a clear and engaging manner that presents complex concepts in a way that can be practically implemented in a variety of areas, including prayer, self-improvement, and setting priorities. He clearly describes the commonality between secular and Jewish approaches to humility, as well as areas where Judaism is distinctly different. Dr. Feiner's humility, self-awareness, and vast Torah knowledge are a potent combination in making this a book that can help lead us to making important changes in our spiritual and emotional lives. I personally have benefited from reading this book as I found myself approaching a number of areas—particularly prayer and my relationship with technology—in a more enlightened and genuine manner.

This foreword highlights the importance of implementing the lessons of this book by briefly summarizing some of the recent research into how technology can impair mindfulness in a manner that impacts on parenting and living a spiritually connected life.

In one of the most replicated experiments in the field of child psychology,[1] University of Massachusetts professor Ed Tronick asked mothers to deliberately be unresponsive to their infants for three minutes, sandwiched by periods of warm interaction. The infants initially responded to their mother's prolonged presentation of a "still face" by actively trying every trick in their repertoire to regain their mother's attention. When these efforts failed, the infants responded with increasingly intense signs of withdrawal, tears, and ultimately hopelessness.

We are hardwired to have strong reactions to being ignored by those close to us. The following story portrays how this dynamic is all too familiar—even in our relationship with older children:

> *A few years ago, I gave a talk on the topic of mindfulness to a group of parents of children facing chronic cognitive or physical challenges. A parent in the audience shared the following story regarding the previous Pesach. His eldest daughter, a nineteen-year-old, seemed intent on stealing the afikomen.[2] He was disappointed in his daughter, thinking that she should have been mature enough to allow her younger siblings a chance to win the prize. Inevitably, the nineteen-year-old was successful, and when the time came for her to negotiate with her father, she asked that he take her out on Wednesday night, leave his smartphone at home, and spend four uninterrupted hours with her.*

---

1   M. Katherine Weinberg and Edward Z. Tronick, "Infant Affective Reactions to the Resumption of Maternal Interaction after the Still-Face," *Child Development* 67, no. 3 (1996): 905–914.

2   A piece of matzah that serves as a dessert at the end of the Seder. It is traditionally hidden during the Seder to be searched for by the children, with a prize given to the one who finds it. This keeps young children interested and motivated during the long proceedings.

The father saw this as an opportunity to reconsider the way he related to his children. He had lost sight of the fact that his children felt abandoned by his smartphone use. He has since made it a regular practice to take his children out, making sure to leave his phone at home. He felt lucky that his daughter hadn't given up on him and was still willing to give him another chance.

———

Almost one thousand years ago, Rabbeinu Bachya ibn Pakuda introduced a short prayer that captures the essence of our objective: "*HaMakom yatzileini mi'pizur ha'nefesh*—May God save me from fragmentation of the soul."[3] We live in a time when many are struggling with *pizur ha'nefesh* (fragmentation of the soul). Recent studies have found that the average American child spends more time using electronic media than going to school. While sixty percent of parents complained that their children were overly dependent on their smartphones, a higher percentage of children (seventy percent) resented their parents' overreliance on their phones.[4]

Perhaps the most crucial area of change attributed to the distracting power of technology is the steady drop in empathy documented in young children.[5] Empathy requires a mindful focus on the needs of others. In a fascinating study illustrating this dynamic,[6] Princeton seminary students were assigned to prepare a speech about the

---

3   *Chovos Halevavos*, Introduction to *Shaar Bitachon*.

4   Michael Robb, "Screenagers: Growing up in the digital age," *Journal of Children and Media* 11, no. 3 (2017): 376–379.

5   Bernd Lachmann, Cornelia Sindermann, Rayna Y. Sariyska, Ruixue Luo, Martin C. Melchers, Benjamin Becker, Andrew J. Cooper, and Christian Montag, "The Role of Empathy and Life Satisfaction in Internet and Smartphone Use Disorder," *Frontiers in Psychology* 9 (2018): 398.

6   John M. Darley and C. Daniel Batson, "'From Jerusalem to Jericho': A study of

Biblical command to help those we see in pain. As the students were walking from one building on the Princeton campus to a neighboring building where they were to be graded on the quality of the sermon, two psychology researchers were waiting for them halfway between the two buildings. One feigned having a heart attack while the other called out to the passing students: "I need help! Can you do CPR?" Some students stopped to help while others rushed off, pretending not to see the sick man.

Waiting for them in the other building were the researchers who asked those who hadn't helped the obvious question: "Why didn't you practice what you were about to preach?" Interestingly, the main predictor of who stopped to help and who evaded their responsibility was how much of a rush they were in. The students who felt stressed and in a hurry were unable to step back and look at the big picture. They were unable to tap into their value system that placed such an emphasis on the importance of helping others.

The importance of not rushing was emphasized by the Baal Shem Tov in his understanding of the words we say several times a day in the Shema, "*V'avadetem meheirah*," which are normally translated as "You will be quickly lost." Out of context, these words can mean "You should lose 'quickness,'" which the Baal Shem Tov homiletically interprets to mean that we should strive to get rid of the rush in our lives.[7] Rushing and not being mindful prevents us from really living with our values.

ATTENTION AND DISTRACTION

Over the last five years, I have been asked to discuss the role of technology with the students of several seminaries in Israel serving

---

situational and dispositional variables in helping behavior," *Journal of Personality and Social Psychology* 27, 1 (1973): 100–108.

7   Rabbi Moshe Tzvi Weinberg, "Maintaining Peace of Mind in a High-Speed World," *Purim To-Go*, 5773, Yeshiva University.

the centrist Orthodox community. I often mention to the students that their teachers find them, collectively, to be much less engaged in the transformative learning and experiential process that in the past had characterized students' Israel studies. The students agree, and they acknowledge that their use of devices has had a significant impact on their ability to focus and become immersed in their learning. Despite this recognition, the students find themselves unable to shed the embrace of devices and to develop the level of independence and growth that in the past has stemmed from the year-in-Israel experience.[8]

The distraction of devices not only impacts academic and intellectual pursuits; it also affects interpersonal relationships. Author and researcher Linda Stone, a former Apple and Microsoft executive, coined a widely used term: "continuous, partial attention." This term captures the feeling of a constant need to be connected to digital devices lest anything be missed. The self-imposed requirement of constant connection mandates an emotional and cognitive state that is always "on." These expectations lead to chronic levels of stress and overload. Typically, one may not even recognize this drain, but interactions with children, spouses, and friends can be subtly tainted by never being fully "present" in day-to-day interactions.

Recent studies have found potential health costs to living with chronic levels of stimulation.[9] The need that many have to chronically check their phones to make sure that they are always responsive to work and social demands can lead to chronic secretion of cortisol, the fight-or-flight hormone that mobilizes our bodies to respond to

---

8   Portions of this section have been adapted from Dr. David Pelcovitz's "Guidelines for Parents in Meeting the Challenge of Digital Technology," *Klal Perspectives*, Fall 2015.

9   Ji-Won Chun, Jihye Choi, Hyun Cho, Mi-Ran Choi, Kook-Jin Ahn, Jung-Seok Choi, and Dai-Jin Kim, "Role of Frontostriatal Connectivity in Adolescents with Excessive Smartphone Use," *Frontiers in Psychiatry* 9 (2018).

danger. While our bodies are designed for sporadic release of cortisol in times of real physical danger, there are documented health and neurological costs when our brains and bodies are constantly primed for crisis.

The subtle way that this dynamic can impact the quality of relationships has emerged in the surprising findings of some recent studies. This research finds that even the presence on a desk of a cell phone that is switched off leads to impairment in attention,[10] as well as a perception on the part of the person being spoken to that the conversation is less meaningful and that the interaction is marked by less empathy.[11]

Psychologist Catherine Steiner-Adair confirms that even newborns are profoundly impacted by a parent's frequent and mindless pull to their digital devices. Paying attention to one's smartphone is qualitatively different than folding laundry or engaging in other superficial tasks. Parents become so engrossed in checking their phones for texts and Facebook updates that they are not psychologically present for their infant or toddlers, whose minds and emotions are being shaped by constantly checking and interacting with their parents. As Steiner-Adair writes: "From birth to two they rely on us completely, and they need our engaged presence during these connecting interactions. They can tell when we are distracted. We can't fool them."[12]

Some recent evidence documents the potential long-term impact that such a lack of mindfulness can have on long-term cognitive

---

10   Bill Thornton, Alyson Faires, Maija Robbins, and Eric Rollins, "The Mere Presence of a Cell Phone May Be Distracting," *Social Psychology* (2014) 479–488.

11   Shalini Misra, Lulu Cheng, Jamie Genevie, and Miao Yuan, "The iPhone Effect: The Quality of In-Person Social Interactions in the Presence of Mobile Devices," *Environment and Behavior* (2016): 275–298.

12   Catherine Steiner-Adair, *The Big Disconnect: Protecting Childhood and Family Relationships in the Digital Age* (New York, Harper-Collins, 2013), 72.

development. Dr. Shonkoff of Harvard's Center on the Developing Child documents the importance of the "serve and return" style of parent-infant conversation. In what he describes as "the conversational duet," Dr. Shonkoff highlights what many of us will recognize as familiar in our exchanges with infants and toddlers. Such conversations are characterized by high-pitched tones, simplified grammar, and exaggerated enthusiasm. Infants exposed to such conversational styles at eleven months and fourteen months know twice as many words at age two as ones whose parents look at their smartphones when interacting with their children.[13] To the extent that language development is a very powerful marker for academic and social success in children, parents should be aware of how crucial it is that they carve out distraction-free interactions with their young children.

In summary, recent research on the pervasive potential impact of technology in our life documents risk to that which we hold most dear—deep connection to others and the ability to raise empathic, caring children who are able to respond to the needs of others with kindness, reciprocity, and empathy.

This book beautifully prescribes the antidote—an approach to mindfulness that is deeply rooted in both Jewish values and secular wisdom.

---

13   Jessa Reed, Kathy Hirsh-Pasek, and Roberta Michnick Golinkoff, "Learning on Hold: Cell Phones Sidetrack Parent-Child Interactions," *Developmental Psychology* (June 2017): 1428.

Acknowledgments

The Hebrew term for gratitude is *"hakaras hatov*—recognizing the good." Sincere gratitude requires awareness and reflection. It requires one to be mindful.

First and foremost, I must thank the source of everything, the source of all good. *"Tov l'hodos LaHashem u'l'zamer l'Shimcha elyon*—It is good to thank God and to sing praise to His exalted name." I thank God for enabling this book to come to fruition. I hope that it can help bring His children closer—to Him and to each other.

When the Talmudic Sages Abaye and Rava were young children, they were sitting in front of their teacher, Rabbah. Rabbah asked them, "When we say the blessing after a meal, to whom are we praying?" They responded, "We are praying to God." Rabbah asked them, "And where is God?" Rava pointed upward toward the ceiling and Abaye went outside and pointed toward the sky.[1]

How are we to understand the different responses of Abaye and Rava? Rabbi Yechezkel Shraga Halberstam explains that although God is the source of everything, we must also thank Him for the many messengers He sends our way. That is represented by the ceiling. Rava pointed to the ceiling to thank God for the parents that He gave him to help throughout life. However, Abaye was unfortunately

---

1   *Berachos* 48a.

XVIII

an orphan—he did not have a ceiling to point to. Therefore, he pointed to the sky.[2]

Fortunately, as I point toward Heaven, I am able to point toward a ceiling. God has provided many messengers to help me along my journey in life and with this book. It would be impossible to acknowledge each messenger individually, but I will try my best to acknowledge those as they relate to this work. I apologize to those whom I may have mistakenly omitted and to those whom I am mentioning but cannot adequately express my gratitude in words.

First, I am grateful to the many *rabbanim* whom I have had the opportunity to learn from, including Rabbi Mendel Blachman, Rabbi Aharon Kahn, Rabbi Yosef Kritz, Rabbi Ahron Silver, Rabbi Baruch Simon, and Rabbi Moshe Stav.

I would like to thank Rabbi Benzion Bamberger, with whom I have the opportunity to learn with and be inspired from; Rabbi Yitzchak Breitowitz, for his guidance, teachings, and beautiful words of blessing; Rabbi Yisroel Saperstein, whose meaningful sermons are concretized in the way he lives; and Rabbi Mayer Twersky, for all that I have learned from him and for the impact he has had on my life.

In chapter 13, "Mindfulness and Mitzvos," we will discuss how mitzvos keep us anchored. There is another important anchor in life—that of a personal *rebbi*. I have been fortunate to have Rabbi Hershel Reichman as a *rebbi*—a role model for what it means to be fully present and accepting of another. Thank you for your assistance with this book and for your constant guidance and encouragement.

Additionally, Rabbi Eytan Feiner is not only my brother, he is also my *rebbi*. He is a tremendous source of inspiration and support. Thank you, Rav Eytan and Rebbetzin Aviva, for everything you have done and continue to do for me. Thank you for being an anchor.

---

2   *Divrei Yechezkel, Likkutim,* cited in the *Mesivta* Gemara.

Relating to my work as a clinical psychologist, I am grateful to Dr. William Sanderson and the faculty of the PhD program at Hofstra University for providing a foundation in studying mindfulness, acceptance, and behavioral change. I thank them for teaching me how to combine professionalism with compassion and how to fuse science with love. I also want to thank my fellow traveler from Hofstra, Rabbi Dr. Benjamin Epstein, for his support and encouragement.

I am grateful to my professional colleagues, friends, and supervisees for helping me keep the beginner's mind and compassion in our work. I specifically want to thank my colleagues at Rockland CBT: Dr. Shlomo Bineth, Mrs. Shaindy Muller, and Mrs. Evi Nakdimen for their feedback, insights, and authenticity.

In addition to learning from colleagues, I learn much from my patients. They continue to deepen my appreciation of the resiliency of the human spirit. Their willingness to be vulnerable for the sake of moving toward values is inspiring. Thank you for letting me be part of your journey.

So many contributed to this work in different ways. Thank you to Rabbi Doron Kornbluth from Mosaica Press for believing in this work, editing it, and guiding it at every stage in the process. Thank you to Rabbi Yaacov Haber and the entire staff at Mosaica Press for their professionalism and expertise in creating the book you are holding. Thank you Mrs. Sherie Gross, managing editor; Mrs. Meira Lawrence, proofreader; and Mrs. Rayzel Broyde for the cover design and typesetting.

Thank you to the following who reviewed different sections of the current work or the original article that it was based on: Dr. Michael Adler, Rabbi Simon Basalely, Meshulem Epstein, Yoav Factor, Yosef Gurevitch, and Rabbi Avraham Union. Ari Muller provided helpful feedback and encouragement. Rabbi Mordechai Nakdimen's expansive knowledge and review of this work clarified many of the important Torah ideas. Mrs. Annie Prager dedicated much time to editing and improving the writing of several chapters. Rabbi Dr. Simcha Willig's incisive feedback helped with the formulation of certain concepts. My brother-in-law and sister, Rabbi and Mrs. Reuven and Shani Taragin (and their children), provided some excellent sources. My brother, Avi Feiner, dedicated time to improving the clarity of certain chapters and provided very helpful guidance along the way.

Much of this book has been inspired from conversations with Rabbi Benzion Brodie and Moshe Zev Lamm. I have learned much from Rav Benzion's authenticity and the way he integrates mindfulness into daily living. Moshe Zev has been a tremendous help with this entire project. His dedication in reviewing the manuscript and sharing insights has been invaluable.

I thank Dr. David Pelcovitz for not only writing the foreword, but for his encouragement at different stages in my personal and professional development. A true leader not only helps the herd as a whole, but watches over the individual sheep.[3] Thank you for everything you do for the community and for individuals.

I am fortunate to have Dr. Yitzi Schechter as a role model, mentor, and friend. I appreciate his guidance and encouragement in this work and in many areas of life. Thank you for teaching me how to live with the fuzziness of this world.

Closer to home, I wish to thank my siblings and my wife's siblings. They are a constant source of love and inspiration. Thank you to my in-laws, Mr. and Mrs. Stan and Karen Fireman, who put so much heart and effort into raising their children. I appreciate their interest, insights, and emotional support in this project and in all of our endeavors.

---

3   See *Shemos Rabbah* 2:2.

I can never fully thank my parents, Dr. and Mrs. Leonard and Bobbee Feiner, for all they have done and continue to do for me. Their unconditional love, selflessness, and dedication to their children is remarkable. Thank you for helping me pave my path in life.

I am eternally grateful to my wife, Romema. Her modesty and the limitations of the written word prevent me from adequately expressing the gratitude she deserves. This work would not have been possible were it not for her *savlanus* and encouragement. Thank you.

"*Hashem oz l'amo yiten, Hashem yevarech es amo ba'shalom*—God will give strength to His nation, God will bless them with peace" (*Tehillim* 29:11).

May we all be blessed with wholeness and peace.

Introduction

As you read these words, try to notice what you are doing. Notice the thoughts going through your mind.

Often, the moment I sit down to read, I am either trying to consume the material as quickly as possible, or I am distracted by everything else occurring in life. Slowing down is challenging. In a world with many noises, distractions, and obligations, it is difficult to be aware of what is taking place right now.

It is easier to live instinctually. But this has consequences. As we strive for speed, we become careless. As we try to connect to everyone, we lose authentic connection. As we prepare for the future, we lose the present. The antidote for such mindlessness is mindfulness—fully paying attention to the present moment.

Mindfulness has gained popularity in the past few decades, both as a way of being and as a formal practice. It was initially introduced to the medical community as a treatment for patients with chronic pain. Patients experiencing physical pain weren't just struggling with the pain itself. Because of the pain, many of the patients avoided activities that were important to them. Some of them engaged in unhealthy behaviors as a distraction from the pain. There was also the added sorrow of not living the life they wished for. In addition to the pain itself, there was the pain of being in pain.

Mindfulness exercises awakened the patients to be more present, both to the pleasant and the not so pleasant—the pain and the beauty of life. They were slowly able to make peace with the physical pain, thereby preventing it from impacting other areas of their lives. The popular mindfulness-based stress reduction (MBSR) program spread around hospitals nationwide and has already helped more than twenty-four thousand people.

During the past forty years, mindfulness has progressed into mainstream science, with research showing that it can be used to treat a variety of emotional difficulties, including depression, anxiety, and anger.[1] It is also used as a tool for enhancing relationships and improving work[2] and athletic performance.

My initial exposure to mindfulness was in graduate school. At that time, mindfulness was slowly becoming a core component of modern psychotherapies, and one of our professors encouraged us to engage in a variety of mindfulness exercises. Although I had previously experienced other forms of meditation, this was different.

Initially, I was not so interested. I found the exercises to be awkward and uncomfortable. The turning point for me was when my professor encouraged us to be mindful about something with which we were struggling. At that time, there was a specific life stressor weighing on me, and as he encouraged us to think about the struggle, I wanted to stop the exercise. I was doing what most people do when confronted with pain: avoidance. However, instead of running away from the pain or fixing it, he encouraged us to observe the pain without fighting it. In staying with the pain, it briefly intensified, but slowly, it became easier. The pain was still there, but I no longer felt the need to escape. In a certain sense, I was able to make peace with it.

---

1   Daphne M. Davis and Jeffrey A. Hayes, "What Are the Benefits of Mindfulness? A Practice Review of Psychotherapy-Related Research," *Psychotherapy* 48, no. 2 (2011): 198.

2   Many of the Fortune 500 companies, including Google and Apple, offer their employees courses in mindfulness.

More than the lectures, and even the science, it was the experience that led me to pursue an interest in not only the academic study of mindfulness, but more importantly, the ability to live more mindfully. As my interest grew, I began to research the Jewish view of mindful practice and living. I was interested in how a Jewish understanding of mindfulness may differ from the secular understanding. This led to an essay entitled "Judaism and Mindfulness: The Value of Being Present," which was written in 2014 as an academic article exploring how mindfulness may be understood from a Jewish perspective.

Although the article clarified some of the issues, it did not suffice as a tool to assist others in living more mindfully. Knowledge is not enough. The book you are holding seeks to be the conduit of taking that knowledge from the head to the heart. We will begin by clarifying a Jewish conceptualization of mindfulness and address potential challenges that Jews may encounter when engaging in mindfulness exercises. We will see how many of the concepts inherent in the secular concept of mindfulness are consistent with Jewish values and can enhance religious observance. We will discuss how to apply these ideas in daily life and how mindfulness is much more than a tool for greater well-being. It is a pathway to authenticity and commitment to values.[3]

Writing can be compared to growing a tree. There is an initial direction you think it's going to take, but it eventually branches into many directions. Although the core of this work will be addressing

---

3   In many ways, the Jewish conceptualization of mindfulness that will be presented is similar to how mindfulness is understood in Acceptance and Commitment Therapy; see Fletcher, Lindsay, and Steven C. Hayes, "Relational frame theory, Acceptance and Commitment Therapy, and a functional analytic definition of mindfulness," *Journal of Rational-Emotive and Cognitive-Behavior Therapy* 23, no. 4 (2005): 315–336.

the interplay of Judaism and mindfulness, we will branch into a variety of topics. Additionally, branches can overlap. Though each chapter has a specific theme, certain ideas will be reexplored through different angles.

As we branch into different topics, we will follow in the path of Rabbeinu Bachya ibn Pakuda, who writes in his introduction to *Chovos Halevavos* that he will "quote the pious and wise men of other nations whose words have reached us...for the Sages have taught: 'Anyone who speaks wisdom—even if he is among the nations of the world—is called a wise man' (*Megillah* 16a)." When examining this wisdom, we will find that much of it can be found within our tradition. The outside wisdom often illuminates wisdom that was already there; we just weren't aware of it—or we weren't paying attention to it.[4]

An essential aspect of mindfulness is being aware of oneself. As we will soon discover, the more we are aware of what is occurring inside us, the easier it is to manage our thoughts and emotions. Therefore, before we proceed further, please allow me to share some of my hesitations.

Before beginning this project, I questioned whether there was a need for this book. To address this, I recalled what Rabbi Shimshon Pincus writes in the beginning of his *sefer* (book) on *tefillah* (prayer). He wonders what he could possibly add to the literature and wisdom that already exists from the sages of previous generations. He responds by stating that each generation has different challenges

---

4   There are also opinions that the wisdom originated from the Torah, but with passing generations it was lost (see *Rema's Toras Ha'olah* 1:11 and *Mishneh Torah, Hilchos Kiddush Ha'chodesh* 17:24). The intriguing topic of Torah, science, and the proper designation of psychological wisdom (philosophy or science) is beyond the scope of this work.

and requires messages tailored for them. Currently, we live in a time when we are bombarded with distractions that pull us away from being present. We live in a time that requires an extra emphasis on being mindful. Therefore, this book was written to help address the challenges of modern life.

To further alleviate this concern, I applied what I respond to clients who think they have no wisdom to offer the world. I share with them the saying of Ben Zoma in *Avos*: "Who is wise? He who learns from every man."[5] The corollary of this statement is that everybody has something to offer. If I am true to my own advice and the words of Ben Zoma, then I must also believe that I have something to offer as well.

In offering these teachings, I am not just a guide; I am also a participant. I am not a mindfulness guru who is in a constant state of equanimity. Indeed, there are many times when I am not as present as I would like to be, but I am trying. I hope we can be fellow travelers on this journey. It is a process—a lifelong process. The ideals in this book clarify what I want to be striving toward. Identifying ideals provides a guiding light.

In clarifying ideals and pathways to reach these ideals, I have gathered from the wisdom of others. This leads to another concern, for although I am not the source of many of the ideas contained herein, they have been filtered through the prism of my mind and thoughts at this moment. There are implicit apprehensions in this. There is the risk that I (the prism) am misinterpreting or distorting another's teaching. There is also the risk that I will look back at this one day and have a different perspective on what was written, because, if a person is growing and changing, his thinking changes. This is probably why some refrain from putting their thoughts into writing—whatever

---

5   *Avos* 4:1.

they think today will be different tomorrow. While there is value in that approach, I chose the other path and hope the benefits outweigh the consequences. Part of the rationale for doing so was because I know that my own life has been enhanced by others' writings. As Rabbeinu Bachya ibn Pakuda writes in his introduction to the *Chovos Halevavos*: "One needs to be careful to not be too careful."

Most of us worry about imperfection—myself included. Writing is one of those endeavors that raises the spotlight on potential imperfections and hence creates some anxiety. Ironically, the very writing of this book and the ideas within have helped me to better manage such worry. I tried to keep in mind Victor Frankl's introduction to *Man's Search for Meaning*:[6]

> *Don't aim at success. The more you aim at it and make it a target, the more you are going to miss it. For success, like happiness, cannot be pursued; it must ensue, and it only does so as the unintended side effect of one's personal dedication to a cause greater than oneself.*

In writing, there is the natural desire to produce a "successful work," but I have tried to make this more than that. In addition to engaging the mind, I hope it can enter your heart and improve your life.

To increase the likelihood of these ideas entering your heart, I encourage you to not only read about mindfulness, but to experience it. To assist with this, many of the chapters conclude with practical suggestions and exercises. (You can find many of these at jmindful. com.) Additionally, I invite you to pause and reflect on what you are

---

6   Vicktor Frankl, *Man's Search for Meaning* (Boston: Beacon Press Books, 1992).

reading—not only on the content but on what is occurring within you. Reflection is the ultimate exercise.

Let us begin the journey.

Note: Most of those whom I have quoted have not reviewed this work. Therefore, I take full responsibility for any misinterpretation. Also, although I tried to provide citations when quoting from others, it could be that an idea that appears to be my own came from something I heard or read and forgot the source. If you think there is anything in need of correction or clarification, please feel free to email RocklandCBT@gmail.com.

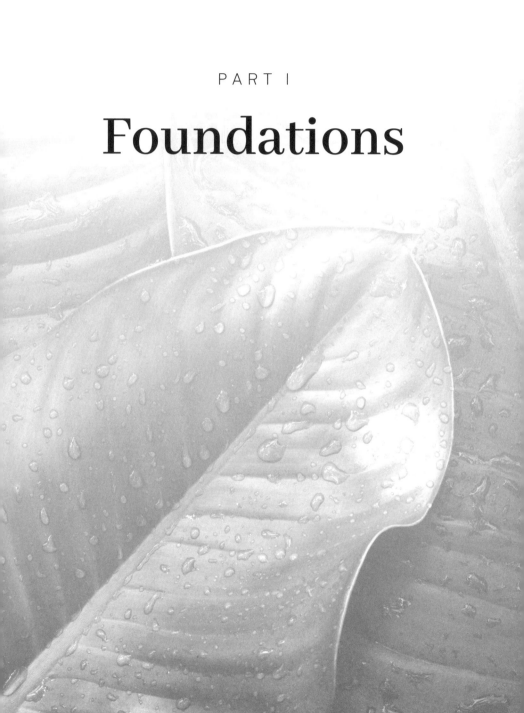

PART I

Foundations

CHAPTER 1

What Is Mindfulness?

A common definition of mindfulness is the process of attending to present-moment experience in a nonjudgmental way.[1] Or, to put it simply, one author noted that the essence of mindfulness is to "notice X." The "X" we are noticing can be anything in the present moment: bodily sensations, a thought, a flower, or a loved one.[2]

However, to convey the essence of mindfulness, we must move beyond words. It must be experienced. Therefore, try to set aside five minutes for the following exercise. You may be tempted to merely read the following paragraph or jump to the next idea. Notice that temptation. Notice the desire to move forward and the difficulty in slowing down. Try to contain the innate desire to "accomplish" or

---

1   Scott R. Bishop, Mark Lau, Shauna Shapiro, Linda Carlson, Nicole D. Anderson, James Carmody, Zindel V. Segal, et al., "Mindfulness: A proposed operational definition." *Clinical Psychology: Science and Practice* 11, no. 3 (2004): 230–241. In addition to the operational definition of mindfulness, Lee Baer and his colleagues at the University of Kentucky conceptualized five different components of mindfulness: the ability to observe experience, describe, detach, love oneself, and act mindfully.

2   Russ Harris, *ACT Made Simple: Second Edition* (New Harbinger, 2019), 40–41.

finish. Try to spend a few minutes paying attention to what is occurring in this moment. Try to pay attention to your current experience.

Let's begin by observing the breath. Notice how it goes in and out. Bring your attention to your diaphragm while you breathe in and out. Notice the way the air feels entering and leaving your body. See if you can stay with the breath for a minute.

Next, try to pay attention to other areas of your body. Slowly, observe each body part from you heart to your toes. Notice if there are any specific areas of discomfort. The goal of this exercise is not to get rid of any discomfort—it is merely to notice what is occurring. If you are experiencing tension somewhere in the body, see if you can pay a little more attention to it. Notice if the sensation changes or moves when you are more aware of it.

Next, see if you can shift your attention to noticing the different sounds in the room. Most of these sounds were occurring before you paid direct attention to them, yet, upon slowing down and noticing them, they become more profound. Similarly, whatever we are paying attention to will usually become more profound as we notice it more.

After a minute of observing sounds, try to notice a different noise. Try to observe the noise of the mind—your thoughts. Imagine there is a cloud above your head containing your thoughts. Notice the stream of thoughts as they flow through your mind. Notice how certain thoughts may have an emotional charge. As certain thoughts show up, you may feel different in your body.

There is no "correct" way to do this exercise. This exercise is about sitting and noticing. If your mind wanders and you stop noticing, that is OK; gently and compassionately, bring your attention back.

Note: Although mindfulness can result in relaxation, this is not the goal. It is not a relaxation exercise; it is an awareness exercise. In fact, there may even be moments of discomfort when doing such an exercise because it can make you more aware of your unpleasant thoughts and sensations. As we will soon discuss, this does not defeat the purpose of the exercise.

After practicing the above exercise, you may ask: What is the point of this? The simple answer is that there is considerable research demonstrating the many benefits of mindfulness, such as managing depression and anxiety, enhancing relationship satisfaction, and improving control of emotional reactivity.[3] Indeed, mindfulness is helpful. However, *why* is it helpful? There is no definitive answer, but we can explore possible mechanisms.

MINDFULNESS OFFERS DISTANCE

Being mindful assists in not taking thoughts too literally. For most of life, we have become accustomed to trusting the mind. For example, if the mind says, "This person doesn't like me," we can easily believe the thought—even if it's not true. We shouldn't always trust our thoughts. The mind can distort reality.

As I was teaching one of my daughters how to ride a bike, I initially held on to the back of the bike and eventually let go. Without realizing that I'd already let go, she said, "Don't let go, I can't ride without you." Even as she was saying that she cannot ride without me, she was riding without me. The mind can tell us we cannot do something, and we can still do it.

Upon being mindful of thoughts, we obtain a distance that enables us to view them more objectively. We can recognize that our thoughts are not necessarily reflective of reality. Holding thoughts and feelings in awareness prevents them from controlling us. For example, one person may be thinking, "I am such a failure and cannot succeed at anything." In contrast, someone else may say, "Right now I am having the thought, *I am a failure*. This thought shows up every now and then, but I don't need to listen to it." The latter is able to notice the thought without being consumed by it.

---

3   Davis and Hayes, "What Are the Benefits of Mindfulness?" *Psychotherapy* 48, no. 2 (2011): 198.

This idea is beautifully described by Rabbi Joseph B. Soloveitchik. He writes:

> *When emotion is raised to the level of experience, we gain the upper hand or control over our own emotions. We acquire the freedom to integrate feelings or to disown them, putting them at a distance from us.*[4]

The very awareness of thoughts and emotions creates a distance between us and our experience. Developing this distance decreases emotional reactivity and frees us from the control of thoughts and feelings. When mindful, we are saved from drowning in the waves of the sea of emotions. We are able to compassionately notice the waves from the safety of the shore. As you read this, try to take a moment and notice the mind. Notice where it is going. Notice how quickly we are pulled into the waves of the mind.

INCREASING ATTENTION TO THE PRESENT MOMENT

A second explanation of how mindfulness improves well-being can be explained with the following exercise.

> Look at the palm of your hand. See if you can notice the different shades of colors, the lines in your hand, the lines within the lines, and any other interesting features. Observe how something as simple as the hand can be so beautiful.

As you were observing your hand, were you engulfed in worries? Were you thinking about your life struggles? Most people report that when they are observing their hand, they are not absorbed in their painful thoughts and feelings—they are absorbed in their hand.

---

4   Joseph B. Soloveitchik, *Out of the Whirlwind: Essays on Mourning, Suffering and the Human Condition* (KTAV Publishing House, 2003), vol. 3, p. 168.

When we fully attend to the present moment, the other noises of life don't take up as much space; they may still be there, but they are not as consuming. Additionally, being present will usually lead to greater efficiency in whatever we are doing and also increase our enjoyment in the current moment. For example, when I am more present with my children, I will be a better father and I will also enjoy the time more. Mindfulness can help us learn to be more present to what is actually in front of us and less in the noise of the past and future—more in the now and less in the mind.

MAKING SPACE FOR EMOTIONS

Another understanding of how mindfulness improves well-being is that it increases tolerance of uncomfortable emotions. Some refer to it as emotional exposure. As humans, we don't like pain; therefore, the immediate response is to try to get rid of it. This can backfire. In many cases, trying to suppress uncomfortable emotions leads to feeling worse.[5] Additionally, the effort to rid ourselves of pain can become more cumbersome than the pain itself. It's like when you are bothered by a buzzing fly in the room. The effort to catch the fly requires more energy than learning to sit with the annoyance of the buzzing. When we allow ourselves to stay with an unpleasant emotion, we'll often see that it becomes more manageable. It also allows the body to process pain in a healthy way.[6]

---

[5]   Laura Campbell-Sills, David H. Barlow, Timothy A. Brown, and Stefan G. Hofmann, "Effects of suppression and acceptance on emotional responses of individuals with anxiety and mood disorders," *Behaviour Research and Therapy* 44, no. 9 (2006): 1251–1263.

[6]   There is a growing literature on the importance of allowing the body to physically process pain, e.g., Bessel Van der Kolk, *The Body Keeps the Score: Brain, Mind, and Body in the Healing of Trauma* (Penguin Books, 2015). As a clinical psychologist, I am often asked why there is an increase in the prevalence of depressive and anxiety disorders. Although there is no absolute answer to this question, one possibility may be that previous generations had fewer distractions, and therefore, when people were in emotional pain, they were forced to stay with it for longer periods of time. This enabled them to process the pain in a healthy manner. Nowadays, when someone is in pain, there are many different

There are times when we convince ourselves that we cannot move forward in life until our pain goes away. One may say, "I cannot speak in public until I get rid of anxiety," "I cannot study until I am in a better mood," "I cannot be a good mother if I am feeling down," etc. This does not need to be the case. We can feel the pain and still move forward. It may be more difficult, but it is possible. A common metaphor used to describe how mindfulness helps manage thoughts and feelings is to think of someone driving a bus with different passengers. Even if the passengers are screaming and telling the driver to go in a certain direction, it is ultimately up to the driver to decide where he wants to go.[7] Similarly, we can slowly learn to treat our thoughts and feelings like passengers. They may be disturbing, but they are not in control. We can learn to make space for them and move forward with doing what is important to us.[8]

SO, WHAT IS MINDFULNESS?

With all this in mind, let us return to the original question: What is mindfulness?

Mindfulness is paying attention. Paying attention to what is happening in this very moment. Observing what is occurring within and without. It is about eating an apple and noticing the way it feels traveling through the mouth and into the body. It is about spending

---

ways that they can distract themselves from it. Distraction can hinder the natural healing process.

7   Steven Hayes, Kirk Strosahl, and Kelly Wilson, *Acceptance and Commitment Therapy: An Experiential Approach to Behavior Change* (New York: Guilford, 1999), 157–158.

8   Throughout the book, we will review this idea of making space for experiences. This is different than how some would define acceptance. Acceptance has a connotation of being OK with something. However, we are often not OK with having unpleasant thoughts and emotions—we don't want them. Making space is about being willing to sit with our experiences for something greater. We can even learn to make space for the part of us that doesn't want to have this thought and feeling.

time with those close to us and fully attending to their words and emotions. It is about observing our own emotions.

Mindfulness is also a way of being. It is a state in which we are able to create distance from our thoughts and sensations and not take them too seriously. As we become more aware of what is in front of us in the present, we can more easily treat thoughts as noises in the background. The noise may be annoying, but it doesn't need to prevent us from living to the fullest right now.

Being present entails facing and accepting reality. When we are able to "be" with what is, we are less troubled with what should be. When we are less consumed with what should be, we are able to appreciate what is.

At times, being present is challenging, especially when emotions are intense. Therefore, it is helpful to practice even when we think it's unnecessary. For example, most baseball players will practice swinging a bat before the actual game so that when the crucial moment arrives, they are better prepared. Similarly, setting aside time to practice mindfulness will assist in being mindful when we may need it most. If we do not apply that which we practice to how we live, we are missing the point.

As I was reading a parenting book, my daughter wanted to show me something. I was about to say, "I'm sorry, can you wait until I finish the paragraph?" Luckily, I caught myself. It's OK to ask a child to wait a few moments, but if I am asking my child to wait so I can read how to be a better parent, then I'm confusing the means and the goal. Similarly, if in reading (or writing) this book, I am pulled away from behaving according to my values, then I am missing the point. If I am not able to apply mindfulness to eating, driving, speaking to people, and prayer, then I am not reaping the full benefits of the time spent cultivating mindfulness.

Mindfulness is more than a good practice; it is a way of life. A way of living that assists in becoming a better person—and a better Jew.

CHAPTER 2

Judaism and Mindfulness — Meeting Points

W here is mindfulness found in Judaism? Everywhere. For some, the term "mindfulness meditation" may be met with reluctance. Perhaps this is because it is often attributed to having origins in Eastern religions. Yet, mindfulness is not only consistent with Jewish practice; it is at the very heart of Judaism. It is not some external concept or addendum. It is part of the very fabric of Jewish living.

Still, since there are many versions of mindfulness around today, we must clarify where a Jewish conceptualization may conflict or converge with those other understandings. As we do, please consider the following points:

- Any attempt to clarify the differences of a construct between two cultures can lead to questioning whether we are addressing the same construct. For example, after recognizing the numerous differences between Jewish prayer and other forms, one may question whether both should be referred to by the same word, prayer. Similarly, in clarifying a Jewish value of mindfulness, we may question whether we should still be using the same term. Nevertheless, for the sake of clarity, we'll use the term mindfulness to describe the Jewish value of being aware in the present moment and its various corollaries.

- Although this book is meant to be a practical guide, you may find this chapter a little more theoretical than the rest of the book. Still, I believe that the following ideas are helpful in setting the foundation for the rest of the book and provide a greater appreciation for a Jewish approach toward mindfulness.

BALANCING THE PRESENT AND FUTURE

One of the challenges with the mind is that it wanders to other places. Staying in the present moment is difficult because we are often thinking about the past or future. How does Judaism approach this tension of dividing our limited resources between the past, present, and future? Let us examine the following passage from *Avos* (2:9):

> [Rabbi Yochanan] said to them: "Which is the proper path to which man should cling?"...Rabbi Shimon says: "He who sees the nolad [i.e., that which is being born]."

In examining the language of the Mishnah, it is important to notice Rabbi Shimon's choice of the *nolad* as opposed to *"ha'asid*—the future." *Nolad* denotes something which is being born, that which is currently in existence.[1] We should focus our resources on the present moment. There is no value in focusing on a future beyond our control. This concept is clarified in the commentary of Rabbi Shimon Bar Tzemach Doron, the *Rashbatz*, on this Mishnah:

---

1   This idea can also be understood from *Rambam*'s commentary on *Avos*, where he states: "Seeing the *nolad* is learning from what is now to what will be."

And this commandment [to see the results of one's actions] does not contradict that which is written in Ben Sirah and Perek Chelek (100b): "Do not worry about the pain of the morrow, for one does not know what the day will bring," and similarly that which is stated in Sotah (48b): "Whoever has bread in his basket and says, 'What will I eat tomorrow,' is of those who have little faith."

[This is no contradiction] because a person should think about the future and do that which he can to save himself from evil; and that which is not within his control, he should have confidence in God and not worry about it.

According to the *Rashbatz*, Rabbi Shimon's message is that we should think about the future regarding that which is within our control. However, for that which is out of our control, we should place our confidence in God and accept. This is similar to the famous Serenity Prayer that is recited at the conclusion of Alcoholics Anonymous meetings:

God, grant me the serenity
to accept the things I cannot change,
courage to change the things I can,
and the wisdom to know the difference.[2]

We can be fully present while simultaneously assessing whether we can impact the future in this moment. For example, if you have

---

2   The Serenity Prayer is attributed to American theologian Reinhold Niebuhr. There is also a Mother Goose rhyme with a similar message:
   For every ailment under the sun
   There is a remedy, or there is none.
   If there be one, try to find it;
   If there be none, never mind it.

a financial difficulty, you evaluate what can be done to improve the situation for the future. However, if it is Shabbos, there is probably nothing that can be done right now. Upon concluding that you cannot change your situation in this very moment, you can subsequently use mindfulness to make space for the unpleasant emotions that arise with the worrisome thoughts. With practice, we can learn to be present and conscious of the *nolad*—if and how we can impact the future in this very moment.

TIME CONSCIOUSNESS

Both Jewish and secular understandings of mindfulness value the importance of being present, while simultaneously considering the past and future. Nevertheless, there may be differences in how to relate to the past and future. For example, Thich Nhat Hanh, an author of numerous texts on mindfulness, writes:

> *The past is already gone, the future is not yet here. There's only one moment for you to live, and that is the present moment.*[3]

I am not sure that Rabbi Soloveitchik would be comfortable with this statement. In his address on "Historical and Individual Mourning," he states:

> *We all know the aphorism, "He-avar ayyin (the past is no more), ve-he-atid adayyin (the future has not yet come), ve-hahoveh ke-heref ayin (the present is fleeting)." However, in my opinion this is wrong. The past is not gone; it is still*

---

3   Thich Nhat Hanh, *The Art of Power* (New York: Harper Collins, 2007), p. 44. Cf., *Sefer Ha'ikarim* of Rabbi Yosef Albo, *maamar* 3:27: "The past is not here, the future has not yet arrived, and the present is the now which is the link between the past and future." Rabbi Albo still recognizes the present as being a link between the past and the future. See also *Pele Yo'etz* by Rabbi Eliezer Papo, *"Da'agah."*

here. The future is not only anticipated, it is already here,
and the present connects the future and the past. That is
what I mean by a unitive time consciousness.[4]

In other words, in Rabbi Soloveitchik's view, we are supposed to focus on the present, but the present includes the past and the future. The importance of viewing the past and future in the present is not purely academic. It can influence how we approach repentance and preparing for the future.[5] To clarify, let us read a selection from Rabbi Soloveitchik's *Halakhic Man*:

Halakhic man is concerned with the image of the past that is
alive and active in the center of his present tempestuous and
clamorous life and with a pulsating throbbing future that
has already been "created." There is a living past and there
is a dead past. There is a future which has not yet been "cre-
ated," and there is a future already in existence…However,
time itself as past appears only as "no more" and as future
appears as "not yet." From this perspective, repentance is an
empty and hollow concept. It is impossible to regret a past
that is already dead, lost in the abyss of oblivion. Similarly,
one cannot make a decision concerning a future that is as yet
"unborn." Therefore, Spinoza [Ethics IV, 54] and Nietzsche
[in Genealogy of Morals]—from this perspective—did

---

4   Soloveitchik, *Out of the Whirlwind*, p. 17. Rabbi Soloveitchik has a similar comment in reference to this saying in his essay "The Community," *Tradition* 17:2 (1978): "Contrary to the popular medieval adage, our story tells of a glorious past that is still real, because it has not vanished, a future which is already here, and a creative present replete with opportunity and challenge. It is a privilege and a pleasure to belong to such a prayerful, charitable, teaching community which feels the breath of eternity."

5   This does not contradict what will be discussed about moving forward from past sins (in chapter 16, "Teshuvah"). Starting anew is important after one engages in proper repentance. Similar to what was said earlier about thinking about the future—if you are able to do something constructive in this moment, do it; if not, put it aside.

well to deride the idea of repentance. However, there is a
past that persists in its existence that does not vanish and
disappear but remains firm in its place. Such a past enters
into the domain of the present and links up with the future.
Similarly, there is a future that is not hidden behind a thick
cloud but reveals itself now in all its beauty and majesty.
Such a future, drawing upon its own hidden roots, infuses
that past with strength and might, vigor and vitality.
Both—past and future are alive; both act and create in the
heart of the present shape the very image of reality. From
this perspective, we neither perceive the past as "no more"
nor the future as "not yet" nor the present as "a fleeting
moment." Rather past, present, future merge and blend to-
gether, and this new three-fold time structure arises before
us adorned with a splendid unity. The past is joined to the
future, and both are reflected in the present.[6]

According to Rabbi Soloveitchik, we do not merely live in the present; we live in what I would refer to as an "expanded present"—a
present where we are to be conscious of our past and our future. This
does not mean to imply that other conceptualizations of mindfulness
disregard the past and the future; still, it seems that Judaism places a
greater emphasis on the past and future.

This is important. Our very identity is rooted in the context of a
greater history. Who we are in the now is related to our history—both
past and future. The bridging of the past and future in the present
is demonstrated in Jewish practice. For example, on Pesach we currently experience the Exodus and speak of the future redemption.
On Shavuos, we not only commemorate the giving of the Torah of

---

6   Joseph B. Soloveitchik, *Halakhic Man*, translated by L. Kaplan (Philadelphia: Jewish
      Publication Society, 1983), pp. 113–114.

the past, but the giving of the Torah today. As Jews, we live in the past, but that is because the past is not gone—it is here, it is now.

History doesn't just provide identity; it provides meaning. When we described mindfulness as noticing what is occurring in the present moment, it is more than just noticing physical sensation or our thoughts. It includes noticing our values.

Being cognizant of the past and future brings meaning into the present. A study examining the differences between meaningfulness and happiness found that a meaningful life requires integrating the past, present, and future, while the happy life is much more present-oriented.[7] A happy and meaningful life requires one to be present, yet see beyond the present.

We say in prayer, "God is the King, God was the King, God will always be the King." Instead of going in chronological order (beginning with "God was the King"), we begin with the present. Why? Because, to be aware of the past and future, we need to first be present.[8] "The past is joined to the future, and both are reflected in the present."

VIEWING THOUGHTS AND FEELINGS NONJUDGMENTALLY

We have seen that a Jewish approach of mindfulness is focused on an "expanded present." Still, mindfulness is not only about attending to the present; it involves an orientation of "attending to present-moment experience in a nonjudgmental way." It involves a conscious decision to abandon one's agenda to have a different experience and a process of "allowing" current thoughts, feelings, and sensations.[9]

---

7   Roy F. Baumeister, Kathleen D. Vohs, Jennifer L. Aaker, and Emily N. Garbinsky, "Some Key Differences between a Happy Life and a Meaningful Life," *The Journal of Positive Psychology* 8, no. 6 (2013): 505–516. The study also found that those who were not as present were not as happy. Many incorrectly assume that happiness and meaningfulness always go together. Although the two are correlated, this study demonstrates that it is possible to have one without the other.

8   Heard from Rabbi Benzion Bamberger.

9   Bishop et al., 233.

For example, from a secular mindfulness perspective, if you notice a thought of being jealous of your friend, you would be encouraged to develop an orientation of acceptance to your thoughts and feelings. This is supported by scientific findings that cognitive and emotional suppression have a rebound effect,[10] and trying to instantaneously suppress a thought and feeling of jealousy is likely to fail.[11]

This aspect of mindfulness may lead some to question: Does Judaism encourage viewing thoughts and feelings in a nonjudgmental manner? In Judaism, we are commanded not to have certain thoughts and feelings; indeed, we have a clear prohibition, "Thou shall not covet" (*Shemos* 20:13).[12] How can we reconcile this with psychological research and practice, which suggests that trying to actively change one's inner experience is often ineffective? I would like to suggest three, non-mutually exclusive, approaches.

Active vs. Passive Thinking

The first approach is differentiating between active vs. passive thinking. *Active thinking* can be understood as a conscious effort to think of specific thoughts. For example, as I write this, I am actively thinking about what I want to write. In solving a math problem, I am purposely calculating specific numbers. Similarly, if I am interested in my friend's car, I can actively think of different ways to obtain his car. In contrast, *passive thinking* occurs when thoughts enter my consciousness without willing them. They are like noises in the

---

10   Jonathan S. Abramowitz., David F. Tolin, and Gordon P. Street, "Paradoxical effects of thought suppression: A meta-analysis of controlled studies, *Clinical Psychology Review* 21, no. 5 (2001): 683–703.

11   This is different than saying that the thought is irrational. As will be discussed in the next few paragraphs, it is helpful to recognize the magnification or irrationality of a specific thought or feeling. Still, recognizing this may not immediately get rid of the thought or feeling.

12   See *Sefer Hachinuch*, mitzvah 416, which clearly states that this mitzvah mandates regulating thoughts and feelings.

background. I don't want them there, but they show up anyway. While we are in control of active thinking, we have very little power on the passive thought processes. In a letter from Rabbi Yisrael Salanter, he writes:

> *If a thought comes against his will, one can be lenient not to consider it a sin. One should not try hard to push aside thoughts, because such is the nature of man; as much as one strives to push away any thought, pain, or something similar, there is a resistance in the psyche of a person to enflame that which is strange to the person. Therefore, excessive striving to push aside thoughts can occasionally create a strong cause to strengthen the thoughts. So too during prayer, much toil to push away unwanted thoughts creates a cause for (more) thoughts.*[13]

Therefore, perhaps we can better understand the prohibition of jealousy and similar commandments related to thoughts and feelings as a mandate to refrain from actively thinking forbidden thoughts.[14] This approach is extremely effective in most cases, but may be very difficult for those struggling with obsessive thinking, because they may still obsess whether their thoughts are truly active or passive. Such individuals may find the following two approaches more helpful.

---

13   *Sefer Igros U'Michtavim* (Letters of Rabbi Yisrael Salanter), Letter #25 (Villman Edition). A parallel scenario in the realm of vision is the prohibition of looking at something inappropriate. If someone flashes an image in your face, there is no transgression (unless you purposely put yourself in such an environment). The challenge with the mind is that it is trickier to differentiate active versus passive thoughts.

14   Cf. *Tanya*, chaps. 12 and 27.

The Heter Approach[15]

In certain cases, one may need to rely on what I refer to as the *heter* approach.[16] This can best be explained using the example of a man struggling with obsessive-compulsive disorder (OCD), who could not stop thinking about worshipping idols during prayer. For years, he tried multiple methods to "control his mind" and "push away these thoughts," yet they only returned in greater intensity. Upon seeing a psychologist, it was explained that the therapeutic method of managing these thoughts is to stop trying to suppress them. Instead, he should learn to get used to the thoughts and even welcome them. Upon consulting his rabbi, he was advised that he is considered a *choleh* (an ill individual), and for treatment, should be told that it is OK to have these thoughts and there is no need to suppress them.[17] Extending this approach to mindfulness would mean that although there is some judgment toward specific thoughts and feelings, there may be circumstances when it is permitted to maintain a nonjudgmental orientation.

Instantaneous vs. Lifelong Objectives

A third approach to managing thoughts is to differentiate between instantaneous mitzvos and lifelong objectives. Many mitzvos can be viewed from a short-term perspective. For example, before eating, we have a mitzvah to say a blessing and, within a few seconds, we have either fulfilled a mitzvah or not. The results of one's actions have an immediate impact since they are short term and time bound.

---

15   A *heter* is the Hebrew term used for permitting that which may have initially been considered forbidden.

16   In treating individuals with obsessive-compulsive disorder, it is advisable to initially use the other two approaches. However, in certain cases, one can depend on the following approach. There is much more to be discussed about this approach from a halachic and clinical perspective, but it would veer us too far from the current subject.

17   Within one week, he had a significant reduction in his obsessions.

In contrast, there are certain mitzvos that can be categorized as lifelong objectives. For example, in reference to the prohibition, "You shall not covet," Rabbi Avraham ibn Ezra explains that a person only covets that which he believes he has access to and that if a person were to recognize that certain objects were truly beyond his reach, he would not be jealous. He describes this with a parable of a peasant who will not desire the daughter of the king because he recognizes that she is beyond his reach.

According to Rabbi Avraham ibn Ezra, jealousy stems from a flawed worldview. If one has such a worldview, they are encouraged to strengthen their belief in God's omniscience. Hopefully, this will reduce the jealousy. Based on this, the mitzvah related to jealousy can be considered a lifelong mission to establish a personality of not being jealous of others.[18] This is accomplished by refining one's mindset through various means, and it is a process. Regulating thoughts and feelings can take time. If I am jealous when I see my friend's possession, thinking of why I should not be jealous may soothe me, but it may not fully get rid of the feeling in the moment. A change in cognition does not automatically lead to a change in emotional reactions.[19]

Although we may not be in control of our immediate thoughts and feelings, we are in control of how we respond to them.[20] We are also

---

18   Rabbi Avraham Ibn Ezra writes in his commentary on *Devarim* 5:18: "The main purpose of all the commandments is to straighten the heart." There is a *shiur* by Rabbi Mayer Twersky that elaborates on this idea of mitzvos being lifelong objectives; see http://torahweb.org/audioFrameset.html#audio=rtwe_12072003.

19   My supervisor from graduate school, Dr. William Sanderson, explained this concept with the following: If someone were to tell you that green lights and red lights were switched so that you are to go on red and stop at a green light, your reactions may not change immediately. It will take a few days to develop the new response of stopping by a green light.

20   This is beautifully elaborated by the *Ramchal* at the end of chap. 7 in the *Mesilas Yesharim*: "One has more control of his outer [movement] than he has over his insides. However,

in control of engaging in studies and behaviors that may influence future experiences of thoughts and feelings.[21] When we experience unpleasant thoughts and feelings in the moment, there is no need for dejection. We can simultaneously be compassionate and judgmental—compassionate in recognizing that unpleasant thoughts and feelings are part of the human condition and it is OK to experience these at times,[22] and judgmental in using thoughts and feelings as a guide for self-examination and putting them in perspective. In fact, when we are mindful, we are better able to distinguish who we truly are from what we are experiencing. Therefore, judging the experience is not a judgment of the self.

To clarify further, when jealousy or other unpleasant emotions arise, there are three possible orientations:

- A judgmental and non-compassionate attitude is: "I am feeling jealous; I must rid myself of that feeling immediately." As stated before, this will probably not work and is more likely to lead to disappointment.
- A nonjudgmental attitude may be: "I am having a thought and feeling of jealousy. Though unpleasant, I can make space for this. A thought is just a thought, and a feeling is just a feeling." This is consistent with many secular mindfulness practices. Though it may lead to greater serenity in the moment, it may not be consistent with halachah.
- A compassionate and judgmental orientation is: "I am having an unpleasant thought and feeling of jealousy. I wish I were already on a level where I did not have such thoughts and

---

if he controls that which he can, he will acquire that which is not in his control." See also *Mishlei* 16:3, and *Rambam, Shemoneh Perakim*, chap. 2.

21   See *Mishneh Torah, Hilchos Isurei Biah* 22:21–22.

22   See *Shabbos* 88b–89a. Moshe Rabbeinu responds to the angels that the Torah was specifically given to mankind because they experience jealousy and other emotions.

feelings, yet I am clearly not there yet. That is OK, since serving God is a lifelong mission. Perhaps I should place more emphasis on studying materials and engaging in behaviors that may decrease these intrusions. But, in this very moment, there may not be much I can do about the thought or feeling."[23]

The mind is an amazing tool, but it can also create problems. The mind helps plan for the future and clarify values, but it can also distort reality and worry about what is beyond our control. Observing the mind judiciously and compassionately can slowly help us use it to work for us, not against us.

⊢————————————————⊣

In summary, the Jewish value of mindfulness differs from the secular conceptualization. If we can be bold enough to develop a Jewish definition for mindfulness, perhaps it can look something like this: Mindfulness is observing the present moment in a compassionate and pragmatic way, viewed in the context of our personal and national spiritual history.

---

23   For some, redirecting the mind away from unpleasant thoughts and feelings may be effective. See *Tanya*, chaps. 26–28, which discusses in more detail how to manage unwanted thoughts and feelings.

CHAPTER 3

The Beginner's Mind

Each day we must start anew. This is an
important principle in serving God.[1]

Rebbe Nachman of Breslov

Before we move further, there is another important aspect
of mindfulness that was not yet addressed: the *beginner's mind*. To have a beginner's mind is a good thing. It
is to observe your experience without the filter of your
assumptions, expectations, and desires.[2] When practicing mindfulness, it is encouraged to observe your experience as if it were the
first time—without the bias of your history—like a child observing
something they've never seen before. This parallels the value of serving God anew each moment.

---

1   *Likutei Moharan* 261.
2   Bishop et al. 233.

RENEWAL

The Baal Shem Tov interprets David HaMelech's plea, "*Al tash-licheini l'eis ziknah*—Do not cast me into old age,"[3] as saying that serving God should not appear old.[4] Practically, how is this achieved? How can we prevent our service from becoming stale? How do we become beginners once again?

One approach is to remember that each day is a new opportunity to serve God as if it were the first time.[5] As we say each day in the morning prayer: "*Ha'mechadesh b'tuvo b'chol yom tamid maaseh v'rei-shis*—He in His goodness renews the world continuously each day." Each moment is a new creation.[6] Each day offers new opportunities that did not exist yesterday and will not exist tomorrow. Although this very moment may appear similar to previous ones, it is not. For example, many find that prayer can become rote. However, recognizing that we will never again have the opportunity to say this prayer in this moment in this place can help to reinvigorate the meaning in it. This moment has never occurred and will never reoccur.

A second way in which mindfulness helps to keep things fresh is by enabling us to become more aware of what is occurring in this moment. When we are more aware, we can recognize that experiences are so vast that even if it appears that we are repeating the same event numerous times, we are not. For example, see if you can reread the line you just read and fully notice what is happening in your mind, body, and the domain of sound. Each time you read it, try

---

3   *Tehillim* 71:9.

4   Baal Shem Tov, *Noach*, 67–68. See *Mishnah Berurah* 61:4.

5   This idea is also found in the verse, "And these words that I command you *today* shall be upon your heart" (*Devarim* 6:6). The *Sifrei* comments: "They should not be to you as an antiquated edict, which no one takes to heart, but like a new one, which all run to read." Similar comments are made on the verses in *Devarim* 11:13 and 27:9. This teaching is repeated numerous times—perhaps because we need to start afresh over and over again.

6   See *Beis Halevi Al HaTorah, Bereishis*. He writes that every moment is a new creation.

to notice a different part of the experience. Heightened awareness of the present moment can lead to a greater appreciation of whatever we are doing. No two moments are the same.

A third pathway for serving God afresh each moment can be explained with a metaphor. If my wife were to say to me, "I would like you to wear a yellow tie so that you think of me more," it will initially have the intended effect. For the first few days of my wearing it, I'd think of her more, but slowly, the effect would fade. Reinvigorating the meaning of the tie by changing to a different-colored or shinier tie would help, but only temporarily. There is another way. Instead of changing the tie, I can think of the relationship itself. If the relationship is real and dynamic, the tie will not require innovation. Reminding ourselves of the relationship with the Divine—the renewed relationship with the Creator each moment—can lead to observing mitzvos with renewed enthusiasm. For example, if we find prayer becoming monotonous, it does not necessarily mean that we need to change the style of prayer. Thinking of the fact that God is in front of us in that moment and that He cares about us can uplift the prayer itself.

RENEWAL OF SELF AND OTHERS

Improving ourselves keeps our relationship with God dynamic. As the individuals in a relationship change, so does the nature of the relationship. Since God does not change,[7] the change must come from within us. If we are the same today as yesterday, then we may, unfortunately, view the world in the same way. But if we change—if we are new today—then our perspectives and relationships are new. The more we grow, the more our experience with God and His Torah will change.

---

7   Although God does not change, the *Nefesh HaChaim* writes (1:7) that the way we behave toward God affects the way He behaves toward us.

I have a sister who teaches in a variety of seminaries in Israel. She tells me that she is able to teach the "same" Torah each year with excitement because the students are always different. Each time she teaches them a specific teaching, it feels like she is teaching it for the first time because, for her students, it is the first. Similarly, if we are constantly changing, then each time we study a specific teaching, we are different from the previous time we studied it. Therefore, our understanding and appreciation of the teaching may be different. This idea applies to prayer as well. Today's prayer should be different than yesterday's because we have changed since then. As Rebbe Nachman states: "If you are not going to be any better tomorrow than you were today, then what need have you for tomorrow?"

If we believe that we can change and grow, then we must believe that others can grow as well. This recognition can increase tolerance of others. If others can grow, then the person I was upset at a month ago may not be the same person today. While it is cognitively easier to label people, this can be harmful. Even good labels can be harmful. Labels reinforce the notion that people are stagnant. Labeling oneself is also unhelpful. Viewing myself righteously can lead to complacency and overconfidence. A negative label can lead to despondence and hopelessness. People change. Each moment can be a new beginning for myself—and for others.

THE WISDOM OF NOT KNOWING

Another application of viewing the world with a beginner's mind is the letting go of preconceived beliefs. We live based on certain assumptions and we create belief systems. This is vital for everyday functioning. Constantly questioning ourselves would make it difficult to make decisions and move forward in life. Still, sticking too strongly to our personal views has its costs. It can prevent us from understanding another's perspective. Because we were each created differently and have been through different life circumstances, it is inevitable that we will have different worldviews.

We should be careful not to treat our subjective beliefs as objective truths. Most foibles in interpersonal relationships stem from assuming that our perspective is the correct one. Our perspective may have validity, but there may be important information missing. There may be a lack in objective knowledge, a lack in fully comprehending the situation, or a lack in understanding the other person and their world.[8] If we can temporarily suspend our view, we will more easily notice what we are missing. We are more likely to understand the view of the other and minimize unhelpful judgments and criticisms.

As you look at the adjacent image, what do you see? Is it a duck? Or maybe it's a rabbit? If you look carefully, you'll notice that it can be viewed as either a duck or rabbit. Being overly fixated on the image of the duck will prevent us from seeing that it can also be a rabbit. To expand our vision, we have to temporarily let go of our immediate perception. We have to be willing to see the image as if we don't already know what it is. This will enable us to recognize the truth in multiple viewpoints.[9]

Ben Zoma states: "Who is wise? He who learns from everyone."[10] He doesn't state that this will *lead* to wisdom; rather, wisdom itself is defined by the ability to learn from others. It is the fool who thinks he knows it all. As Shlomo HaMelech writes: "A conceited fool has no desire for understanding, but only wants to

---

8   This idea is adapted from Rabbi Aharon Lichtenstein's essay on *Daat Torah*.

9   Recognizing the truth in multiple viewpoints is not only important to maintaining successful relationships, but it is a core principle in *talmud Torah* and the halachic process. As it states in *Bamidbar Rabbah* (13:16): "There are seventy faces to Torah."

10   *Avos* 4:1.

express his own view."[11] This relates to a phenomenon referred to as the Earned Dogmatism Effect, which demonstrates that self-perception of high expertise increases dogmatism and closed-mindedness.[12] The key word is self-perception; the more one thinks he is an expert, the less open he will be to a variety of opinions. "Do you see a man who is wise in his own eyes? For a fool there is more hope than for him."[13] Wisdom requires humility and recognizing limitations.[14]

Let us try to cultivate the beginner's mind. To be willing to "know" a little less and to be willing to learn from others.

Let us try to view this moment as if it is the first and be amazed with the world God creates each and every moment.

T R Y

1. Observe how a young child explores the world. Notice how they view objects with a certain curiosity. Observe how they play with objects not knowing what they are and what they are for. Try to view an object like a child would.

2. Look around the room and observe your surroundings. See if you can notice aspects of the room that were previously ignored (e.g., the shadows of the objects, the way the light reflects throughout the room, the variety of colors, etc.).

3. Reflect how each aspect of your experience only exists because of the will of God. It is in His power to cease existence

---

11   *Mishlei* 18:12.

12   Victor Ottati, Erika D. Price, Chase Wilson, and Nathanael Sumaktoyo, "When Self-Perceptions of Expertise Increase Closed-Minded Cognition: The Earned Dogmatism Effect," *Journal of Experimental Social Psychology* 61 (2015): 131–138.

13   *Mishlei* 26:12.

14   This can explain why some of the forty-eight *kinyanim* (tools of acquisition) of Torah (*Avos* 6:6) include characteristics such as humility, not taking credit for one's achievements, loving mankind, and judging one's friends favorably.

and in His power to sustain it. Each moment and object exists because of His will.

4. Take a few moments to reflect on your own assumptions and beliefs about the world. Notice how so much of the way we live is based on specific assumptions. See if you can be willing to question one of these assumptions.

5. As you continue reading, try to maintain an open mind—a beginner's mind. Notice how the mind judges the written word, either in agreement or disagreement. Before the mind arrives at its conclusion, try to hold it in awareness a few moments longer.

CHAPTER 4

Discovering the Self

Just as a person is obligated to believe in
God, so too, he must believe in himself.[1]

Rabbi Tzadok HaKohen

At the very moment a man finds himself,
he finds God.[2]

Kierkegaard

U pon introducing the concept of mindfulness to a
client and discussing the concept that we are not our
thoughts, he asked, "If I am not my thoughts, then
who am I?"

---

1   *Tzidkas Hatzaddik* 154.
2   Rabbi Soloveitchik quotes this line in *Vision and Leadership* (KTAV Publishing House,
     2012), p. 76.

I responded, "You are the one who is noticing your thoughts."
He asked, "What's that?"

—————————————

Who are you? What makes you *you*?

Are you your body? Possibly, but if parts of your body were not here, you would still be you.

Are you your thoughts? While your thoughts may be part of your experience, they are constantly shifting.

Your truest self is the part that notices your experience.[3] It is the *neshamah* (soul).[4]

Rabbi Shimon ben Pazi states:

> *The five verses of Barchi Nafshi, regarding whom did [King] David state them? He stated them regarding none other than the Holy One Blessed Be He and regarding the neshamah. Just as the Holy One Blessed Be He fills all the world, so too does the neshamah fill all the body.* **Just as the Holy One Blessed Be He observes but is not observed, so too the neshamah observes, but is not observed.** *Just as the Holy One sustains the world, so too does the neshamah sustain the body. Just as the Holy One is pure, so too the neshamah is pure...*[5]

---

3   Contextual behavioral science literature refers to this as the "noticing self" or the "observer self."

4   I initially hesitated writing this chapter because of my lack of familiarity with the Kabbalistic understandings of the different levels of the self (e.g., *ruach, chayah, yechidah*). Although I recognize this chapter is oversimplifying complex topics, I hope the benefits outweigh the consequences. I also take comfort in the recognition that most of what is written by the human mind simplifies complex realities.

5   *Berachos* 10a.

The *neshamah* observes, but is not observed. It notices experience, yet cannot be noticed itself. When we are mindful and observing our experience, we are more in touch with the *neshamah*.[6]

We say in the prayer of *Elokai Neshamah*, "God, the *neshamah* that You gave me is pure." The body may sin and thoughts may go to disturbing places, but the *neshamah* is always safe. Think of a newborn child. There is something beautiful and Divine with the child itself. The child didn't do anything specific to deserve love, but we love the child anyway. Inside each of us is something beautiful and Divine. Unfortunately, we are easily pulled away from that part of ourselves.

NESHAMAH—THE PLACE OF CHOICE
Rebbe Nachman of Breslov writes:

> *The primary part of a person, the I, is the neshamah, which is everlasting. It is because of the brazenness of man and his desires that the neshamah, the essence of man, is distanced from the body. It is through the yearning and*

---

6   Rabbi Shimon ben Pazi's statement describes the *neshamah* as modeling God. Interestingly, Rabbi Jeremy Kagan (*Dialogue*, no. 7, p. 164) discusses how through his recognition of his true self, he was able to strengthen his belief in God. He writes:

> My path to *emunah* began from extrapolating from my internal experience. The only thing which I know "as it is" (in its being) as opposed to how it merely appears is my own being or self. Though my self has a physical component as well as a non-physical dimension, I experience that physical aspect as the vessel of my non-physical consciousness. I identify with my inner experience along with its history. That is I; it is who I am. That means that one hundred percent of my sample of "being" is an internal spiritual entity which merely takes on expression through its physical vessel. Therefore, the most logical starting point to understand reality is to assume, unless proven otherwise, that the "being" of all things consists of hidden, spiritual cores—even those that I can only access through their physical appearance. That is, it is most logical to assume that just as my "being" is a spiritual, inner dimension, so also everything besides my self must have a similar "being." And if I perceive existence as a unified whole, it also must have an essence. Though God is much more than the essence of creation, this thought process brings one a long way down the path toward recognizing His existence.

*striving for holiness in which a person reunifies the body
and neshamah.*[7]

According to Rebbe Nachman, the *neshamah* is the truest self. It is
the part of us that has the capacity of choice. The *neshamah* chooses
which thoughts to respond to, which limbs to move, and what words
to say. Therefore, utilizing free choice is the greatest form of self-ac-
tualization. Choosing to go against the natural force of what is easier
and turning instead to a more difficult yet meaningful choice demonstrates that the *neshamah* is in control. This is what separates us from
animals. This is what makes us who we are. The crowning glory of
man is the utilization of free choice in a meaningful direction. The
capacity of choice is where we find the real I.

NESHAMAH—THE PLACE OF OBSERVATION

The *neshamah* observes, but is not observed. Observing experience enables us to better live in the expanded present (see chapter
2). It helps us recognize that this very moment is but one piece in our
greater history. In the words of Rabbi Jonathan Sacks:

> *Though we are part of nature—we have bodies, we feel
> hunger and cold, we age and die—there is something within
> us that is not part of nature, namely self-consciousness,
> the ability to stand back from our immediate situation and
> pass judgment on it. The Greeks called this "the soul." The
> second chapter of Genesis calls it "the breath of God." The
> combination of language and self-consciousness means that
> human beings have a sense of time to be found nowhere
> else in creation. All animals have a sense of cyclical time
> hardwired into their brains. Some migrate; others hibernate
> at particular points in the year. What is unique to humans*

---

7   *Likutei Moharan* 22.

is the sense of a distant past and future: "there was" and
"there will be." It took a radical imaginative leap to see that
if we are free, not wholly determined by nature, the world
of "there will be" might be altogether different from that of
"there was."[8]

The ability to observe our thoughts and feelings is what differentiates us from animals. Being mindful enables us to bring the past and future into the present; this brings meaning into our lives (see chapter 2).

THE REAL "I"

Mindfulness, the ability to notice experience, provides perspective. It helps us recognize that we are not our experience; there is a deeper "I" that observes experience. We are not entirely defined by our actions. There is an "I" that observes actions. There is a part of us, the *neshamah*, that is OK just being. Recognizing that we have value independent of our actions limits disappointment in apparent failures—and arrogance in supposed success.

This insight clarifies a teaching by Rabbi Chaim Vital. He writes that anger and arrogance are essentially one trait that stems from the *yesod* (foundation) of fire.[9]

What does this mean?

It is the nature of fire to begin from an initial powerful source and spread. When it spreads too far, it is destructive. Similarly, our beings stem from an initial source, the *neshamah*. Like fire, we too can spread away from our source. We can fail to recognize the boundary between our real selves (the source) and what we sometimes refer to as "me" (external qualities).

---

8   Jonathan Sacks, *The Jonathan Sacks Haggada* (Jerusalem: Maggid Books, 2013), p. 97.

9   *Shaarei Kedushah* 1:2.

For example, if I am driving a limousine for a car service, I would be foolish to take it personally when others compliment the car. I would also be foolish to be offended when others insult the limousine. I am not the car. I am not even the owner—I am the driver. Both arrogance and anger stem from believing that we are the owners of our bodies. In reality, we are drivers of the body we encapsulate, the lives we encapsulate. It is easy to blur the lines of who we really are. Our body and current lives are the vehicle that we use to fulfill the will of God, but ultimately, these are not our truest self.

The true self is the *neshamah*. This realization can be liberating. Remembering who we really are can free us from the disappointments in life and can help us focus on being the best drivers we can be.

T R Y

Note: Many of the mindfulness exercises begin with noticing the breath and the body because they are usually the easiest to notice. Awareness of the breath helps ground us in the present moment. Upon staying with the breath for a few moments, it is usually easier to notice other parts of experience.

1. Notice your breath. Remind yourself of the verse, "God breathed into man."[10] The breath is your anchor. It is the part of you that is secure, independent of whatever else is occurring in life. Notice the different parts of your experience. Notice the body, sounds, and thoughts. Notice who's noticing. There is a part of you that is deeper than your experience.

2. Think of yourself as a child. Who's noticing that child? You. If you are noticing, then who is the child? Try to picture yourself ten minutes ago. Who's noticing that?

---

10   *Bereishis* 2:7.

CHAPTER 5

Being and Doing—Part I

I n the midst of a serious life challenge, we can believe that if only the crisis did not exist, we would be at peace. In the midst of the crisis, we may find it unfathomable how those who are not experiencing such a crisis can be so shallow and not appreciate what they have. Yet, even when we are not at such depths of suffering, pain has its way of finding us. We can still experience the pain of insignificance and of not finding satisfaction in day-to-day life.

We live in an era in which we are prone to easily feeling insignificant. Immediate exposure (through the ever-present media and Internet) to anything that is happening anywhere makes it easy to compare ourselves to anyone and everyone. The moment we open a news site, we are inundated with stories of the "successful others," those who have "made it." If we were to personally know them, we would recognize that they too have struggles. But we only see them from afar. From a distance, it appears like they have it all—and that we don't.

Mindfulness is a partial solution to such pain. It helps us cultivate self-acceptance, which we will define as finding significance in *being* and *doing*.

- Finding meaning in being results from reminding ourselves that we all have worth—independent of our actions. As we discussed in the previous chapter, we are all created as beautiful souls and have value in our very existence. Like a newborn child, we are special and valuable just for being.
- At the same time, we are also charged with doing, and we need to find meaning in that as well.

For some, this may lead to confusion. If I am worthy for just being, do I really need to do? On the other hand, if I need to do, then how am I OK for just being?

The following metaphor can clarify: If I own a beautiful diamond, I will seek to maintain its beauty by guarding it from contamination, and I will try to add to its beauty by polishing it and doing whatever possible to uncover its luster. I can also choose to mistreat the diamond and dirty it. The beautiful one is preferable, but the sullied diamond is still a diamond, and still has worth.

Worth is based on *both* being and doing:

- There is a part of us that is valuable for merely existing. The fact that we were created by God and created in His image makes us a diamond. God would not have placed us here if He did not deem us valuable.
- Still, it is up to us what we do with the diamond. Positive actions increase the beauty of the diamond and negative actions taint it. Acceptance is not an excuse to live an idle life. We are charged with beautifying the diamond.[1]

---

1   This idea and the following discussion are beautifully described by the Chazon Ish. He writes:

Correction of one's character does not negate self-love; the existence of tendencies toward pleasure and honor is a positive component of the creature called man. Negating these tendencies does not build up man's soul, but rather destroys it. *Mussar* tells a person: Love yourself and acquire honor and respect, but know where your true happiness in the world stems from, and what your true source of honor is: true honor

Recognizing the inner value of the diamond leads to a greater desire to beautify it. As the psychologist Carl Rogers noted, "The curious paradox is that when I accept myself as I am, then I change."[2] We can learn to both be and do.[3]

CULTIVATING BEING

Finding peace in being requires love. Our sense of self is built on the unconditional love and acceptance we initially received from another. Although we can cognitively remind ourselves that we have value in being, the logic can only go so far. It cannot compare to the actual experience of being loved. Hopefully, one will have received this as a child. But, even if one did not, it can be healed in the present through healthy relationships, oneself, and the recognition of God's love for us.

It is tempting to fulfill the innate need for acceptance by pursuing honor.[4] Honor provides a powerful dose of what acceptance and love feels like. Therefore, it can feel very good. But the good feeling from honor fades and there arises the desire for more. It can become a drug. It is never satisfied. Honor cannot bring lasting peace because it derives from without. Self-acceptance—what we dream honor may deliver—comes from within.[5]

---

lies in Torah; true honor lies in humility; true honor lies in abandoning honor; true happiness lies in liberating oneself from natural tendencies, and subjecting oneself to God and to His Torah—the goal of life both in this world and in the next. (4:14; translation adapted from *Faith and Trust*, translated by Yaakov Goldstein)

2   Carl Rogers, *On Becoming a Person: A Therapist's View of Psychotherapy* (Houghton Mifflin Harcourt, 1995), p. 17.

3   Or, as my Israeli nephew quipped, we must learn to be like a teddy bear, whose Hebrew translation is *doo-be*.

4   We will be defining honor as being highly respected by others (as opposed to a healthy honor like that mentioned by the Chazon Ish).

5   This line is adapted from Alan Block's *Pedagogy, Religion, and Practice* (Palgrave Macmillan, 2007). He writes: "Reputation always derives from without; but contentment, what I dream reputation might deliver, comes from within" (p. 170).

BECOMING SOMEONE

For too long, I thought I needed to be "someone" to be someone.

Of course, this view is incorrect; we all have worth independent of what we produce. Recognizing the fallacy of such thinking is helpful, but the feelings may still show up. We need not completely ignore such feelings. Aspirations motivate. We have an innate desire to produce, accomplish, and contribute to others. More than the calf wants to suckle, the cow wants to nurse.[6] Still, it would be foolish to expect the external approval we may receive from our accomplishments to bring equanimity. It may feel good temporarily, but it will not lead to genuine happiness.

An alternative to pursuing honor is pursuing values. It may not provide the immediate pleasure of honor but will more likely provide long-term equanimity. "There are many thoughts in man's heart, but the advice of God will stand" (*Mishlei* 19:21). Man has many ideas of what will be best for him, but it is following the word of God that produces true eternity.[7]

True worth is not dependent on others' praise. Thinking of the unethical public figures who receive praise and admiration clearly demonstrates that honor is not synonymous with worth. Rather, the true worth in doing stems from living according to our values—this brings eternity.

MEANING IN DOING

While pursuing values is important, it is possible to live a life of pursuing values and still feel insignificant. Life can become so rote that we forget what we are pursuing. Not being cognizant of the value in the doing will lead to becoming frustrated with the journey. For example, people can be engaged in many meaningful

---

6   *Pesachim* 112a.
7   See the introduction of *Shem Olam* by Rabbi Yisrael Meir Kagan (the Chafetz Chaim).

activities—working, spending time with family, prayer, etc.—and forget why they are doing what they are doing. This is where mindfulness comes in. Being mindful of why we are doing what we are doing uplifts the journey itself. Finding spirituality in the *now* helps us find peace in this moment.

Rabbi Eliyahu Eliezer Dessler writes:

> *Those who during their lifetime are attached to true spirituality now experience a fullness of being. "Those who love Me will inherit being" (Mishlei 8:21). Their being in this world is entirely within themselves and in no way dependent on anything outside themselves. They are therefore capable of being completely happy with their lot. One who desires something outside himself thereby destroys his true self. Hillel said, "If I am not for myself who is for me?" Meaning, what have I to hope for if I am not in possession of my true self?*[8]

Recognizing that in this very moment, we are living the way we are supposed to live can lead to a sense of serenity. For this to happen, there must be an a priori recognition of what it means to be living a meaningful life.

THE VALUE OF EFFORT

Spiritual success cannot be measured with the standards of the physical world. Recently, I saw a billboard advertising a hospital. On the ad was a picture of football coach Bill Parcells stating, "You don't get medals for trying, you get medals for results." Society tells us that success is measured by results. It tells us that if we cannot produce tangible results, we are failures.

---

8   Rabbi Eliyahu E. Dessler, *Strive for Truth! Michtav Me'Eliyahu: Selected Writings of Rabbi E.E. Dessler*, vol. 4. (Feldheim Publishers, 2002).

It is easy to forget the true barometer for success. At times, it can be difficult finding satisfaction in the present moment because we fail to see the meaning in the process. We can become overly focused on the outcomes of our efforts. Producing results can gain attention and honor (temporary acceptance), but it is short-lived.

External "achievements" do not define our status. True achievement is based on doing our best in this very moment. It is based on our effort.[9]

The Talmud relates that Rabbi Yosef briefly passed away, but was soon revived. Upon his revival, his father asked him what he saw during his brief journey in Heaven. Rabbi Yosef answered, "I saw an upside-down world. I saw upper ones below and lower ones above."[10]

The seemingly successful in this world may not be as high in the next, and the apparent failures in this world may be higher than expected. We don't truly know who is higher and who is lower. What is considered valuable in this world differs from what is valuable in the world of truth.

> *Someone came to Rabbi Elyashiv complaining that throughout his lifetime he had worked hard to elevate himself in avodas Hashem (serving God) but with very little to show for all his efforts. He remarked, "I am afraid that all it will say on my tombstone is, "Here lies someone who tried."*
>
> *Rabbi Elyashiv responded, "If I were walking in a cemetery and saw a tombstone with such an inscription, I would stop and pray at the grave of the tzaddik."[11]*

---

9   Spiritual achievement isn't just about positive behaviors. In Rabbi Aaron Lopiansky's *sefer, Ben Torah for Life,* he discusses how the very action of refraining from negative is an amazing spiritual accomplishment (see the chapter, "Doing by Not Doing").

10   *Pesachim* 50a.

11   Adapted from Rabbi Binyomin Forst's chapter in *Step by Step* (Shaar Press, 2012), "Tolerance."

In the world of truth, medals are not awarded for results—they are awarded for effort.

T R Y :

1. Set aside a few minutes to sit with yourself—your entire self. Your thoughts, feelings, sensations. It's OK to let yourself just be. Notice what shows up. You don't need to run away from yourself. You are OK in this moment. David HaMelech wrote, "*B'tzar hirchavta li*—In my distress, you have expanded me" (*Tehillim* 4:2). We ask to be able to expand ourselves. When we expand ourselves, we realize that we can contain much more than we think we can—we can contain our entire experience—all the different parts of ourselves (see chapter 18, "Authenticity and Wholeness").

2. Think of a newborn baby. Imagine what it would be like caring for that baby. Imagine the love the parents would feel toward that baby. Next, try to redirect that love toward you. There is a part inside of you that is pure, just like that baby. You are deserving of love just like anyone else. You are God's beautiful child. Even though you have flaws and imperfections, you are still a beautiful diamond.

3. The next time you are around people, try to see their inner beauty. Remind yourself that they too are diamonds. They were once beautiful children that somebody loved. Being more compassionate of others leads to being more compassionate of oneself. It works both ways.[12]

---

12 See the *Tiferes Yisrael* commentary on *Avos* 2:9. He states: "The person with an *ayin ra* (evil eye) has a negative outlook of life. He is not happy with that which he has and he looks at others negatively." It goes together.

4. If you are going through a challenging time in life, try to set aside time to notice your pain. Try to break it into smaller pieces. Where do you feel it in the body? What are the painful thoughts showing up? See if you can stay with the experience without trying to fix it. As you do, remind yourself that God loves you. Remind yourself that there are other people in your life who love you. **Love provides the foundation for managing life's challenges.**

CHAPTER 6

Being and Doing — Part II

I received the following email from a former patient:

Hi Dr. Feiner,

I've been going to a class on mindfulness. The class spends most of the time on quiet meditations, body scans, and yoga exercises. The ideology seems similar to some of what we discussed in therapy, but here, we are spending literally forty-five minutes noticing the breath! In your opinion, is this necessary/helpful?

As mindfulness increases in popularity, so do the number of classes, seminars, and extended mindfulness retreats. The question arises: How much time should be spent in formal mindfulness exercises? How much time do we spend in the *being* mode?

Like physical exercise, more is usually better, but this does not mean we should exercise all day. Currently, the research is unclear as to what is the necessary dose of mindfulness to produce positive effects.[1] Although there is tremendous value in immersing oneself in

---

1   James Carmody and Ruth A. Baer, "How long does a mindfulness-based stress reduction

mindfulness meditations and the being mode, like most things in life, it needs to be balanced. Time is limited: *"Ha'yom katzar v'ha'melachah merubah*—The day is short and there is a lot of work."[2] We need to balance the being mode and doing mode. Like a tree, we can be beautiful the way we are—but we still need to grow.

FINDING YOUR JOURNEY

Gil Locks, the Central Park guru who became an Old City Jew, remarked that upon seeing a flower there are three possible responses:

- The Westerner will take the flower for himself.
- Someone from an Eastern philosophy will observe the flower in an effort to detach and transcend.
- The Jew will water the flower.

Our goal is not to detach from the world—it is to uplift the world. We have to "do." The question then arises: What are we supposed to do? In other words, what are we living for? It is a shame to live mindlessly.

"Some men fish all their lives without knowing it is not really the fish they are after."[3] What are we after? Even if we do not find clear answers, we should at least start by asking the questions.

STAYING ON COURSE

Years ago, my father shared with me the following story:

> *An American investment banker was at the pier of a small coastal Mexican village when a small boat with just one fisherman docked. Inside the small boat were several large yellowfin tuna. The American complimented the Mexican*

---

2   program need to be? A review of class contact hours and effect sizes for psychological distress," *Journal of Clinical Psychology* 65, no. 6 (2009): 627–638.

2   *Avos* 2:20.

3   I have seen others attribute this quotation to Thoreau, but I was unable to find the original source.

on the quality of his fish and asked how long it took to catch them.

The Mexican replied, "Only a little while." The American then asked why he didn't stay out longer and catch more fish. The Mexican said he had enough to support his family's immediate needs. The American then asked, "But what do you do with the rest of your time?"

The Mexican fisherman said, "I sleep late, fish a little, play with my children, take siestas with my wife, stroll into the village each evening where I sip wine, and play guitar with my amigos. I have a full and busy life." The American scoffed, "I am a Harvard MBA and could help you. You should spend more time fishing and with the proceeds, buy a bigger boat. With the proceeds from the bigger boat, you could buy several boats, and eventually you would have a fleet of fishing boats. Instead of selling your catch to a middleman, you would sell directly to the processor, eventually opening your own cannery. You would control the product, processing, and distribution. You would need to leave this small coastal fishing village and move to Mexico City, then LA, and eventually New York City, where you would run your expanding enterprise."

The Mexican fisherman asked, "But, how long would all this take?"

To which the American replied, "Fifteen to twenty years."

"But, what then?" asked the Mexican.

The American laughed and said, "That's the best part. When the time is right, you would announce an IPO and sell your company stock to the public and become very rich—you would make millions!"

"Millions—then what?"

The American said, "Then you would retire. Move to a small coastal fishing village where you would sleep late, fish a little, play with your kids, take siestas with your wife, stroll to the village in the evenings, where you could sip wine and play your guitar with your amigos."[4]

This story is both humorous and sad. Sad, because there are times when we act like the American businessman. There are times when we incorrectly sacrifice today for a wealthier tomorrow. The world can easily pull us away from our values and we can forget what we're really after.

THE GOOD LIFE

What are people after? Surveys show that many young adults believe that fame and wealth are the ingredients for a good life. Though many recognize the error in this belief, others unfortunately continue to believe in this delusion. In one of the longest studies in history, the Harvard Study of Adult Development, a picture was formed of the factors predicting long-term happiness. Beginning in 1938, researchers tracked the lives of over seven hundred men and discovered that the quality of relationships is the best predictor of happiness and health. Having close, warm, and dependable relationships were correlated with improved physical, mental, and emotional health.

Robert Waldinger, the Study's current director, asks, "Why is this so hard to get and so easy to ignore?" He answers, "What we'd really like is a quick fix, something we can get that'll make our lives good and keep them that way. Relationships are messy and they're

---

4   In researching the origin of the story, it appears that it's a common adaptation from a short story published by a German writer, Heinrich Böll, in 1963.

complicated."[5] Sometimes, trekking through the messy and complicated is the better path.

Most species respond to whatever provides the most immediate reinforcement. Money is a powerful reinforcer. Since it feels good, we are naturally pulled toward it. But, as the Harvard study shows, responding to immediate reinforcement is not always in our best interest. As humans, we are charged with rising above the natural state. To do this, we need to pause and reflect; we need to be mindful.

CHESHBON HANEFESH (ACCOUNTING OF THE SOUL)

By giving ourselves time to be, we can discover what we need to do.

The *Ramchal* in *Mesilas Yesharim* explains that Pharaoh was able to enslave B'nei Yisrael in Egypt for so many years by keeping them perpetually busy. This prevented them from having time to pause and reflect on their wretched circumstances.[6] Slowing down the autopilot mode enables us to pause and ask what is important.[7]

The *Ramchal* concludes his chapter on *zehirus* (watchfulness) with the following:

> *A person must constantly contemplate with his mind and also set aside fixed times to reflect what is the correct path to follow, according to the Torah. Afterward, he should contemplate his deeds to see if they are on the correct path or not.[8]*

The mindful Jew does not merely pause to pay attention to the present moment.

---

5   Found at https://robertwaldinger.com/ted-talk/.
6   *Mesilas Yesharim*, chap. 2.
7   One of the reasons why we encourage children to ask so many questions on the night of the Seder is because questions lead us back to God. Questions demonstrate that we are not acting on autopilot; rather, we are thinking and analyzing what we are doing.
8   *Mesilas Yesharim*, chap. 3.

The mindful Jew also pauses to clarify his values and to reflect how he can better live according to these values.

The verse states: "You shall appoint judges and officers by all of your gates." The *Sfas Emes* teaches that "judges" (*shoftim*) refers to the clarification of values—the intellectual recognition of what is correct and what is not, and that officers (*shotrim*) refers to the behavioral manifestation of the knowledge.

Most people err in one of these areas. Either they are not honest with themselves in clarifying what is correct, or they know what is right but do not follow through with it. Setting aside time to clarify values reminds a person what is important to them and helps them bring it into the present moment.

Indeed, we were created as beings that require self-reflection. It is embedded in the very nature of the world. As Rabbi Aaron Lopiansky writes:

> We could present many proofs for this, from the many pe-
> sukim speaking about our mindless rush "like a horse in bat-
> tle" (Yirmiyahu 8:6) to the Chovos Halevavos's concept of
> cheshbon hanefesh to the baalei mussar who made seclusion
> and cheshbon hanefesh the cornerstone of their method.
>
> I believe that the ultimate source for this is Hashem's
> interaction with our world. The Gemara (Rosh Hashanah
> 16a) teaches us that there are yearly, daily, and moment-to-
> moment examinations and judgments of the world. As with
> all of G-d's actions, these constant assessments do not so
> much describe a Divine need as they describe a paradigm for
> us to emulate. We need to regularly set times for reviewing
> and analyzing our course.[9]

---

9   Rabbi Aaron Lopiansky, *Ben Torah for Life* (Eshel Publications, 2018), p. 124.

REDEFINING DOING

Cheshbon hanefesh, setting aside time to reflect, helps us discover what we value. But it is not enough to clarify values as something to strive for. We need to concretize values in this very moment. We don't want to fall into the trap of sacrificing what we should be doing in the moment for some "greater" value. For example, a common obstacle to *shalom bayis*, peace in the home, is the rationalization of inappropriate behavior for a greater good, such as criticizing one's spouse because they will not make it to an event on time or ignoring one's family in order to be more involved in *chessed* projects.

In Rabbi Shlomo Wolbe's *Kuntres Hadrachah L'Chasanim*, he quotes the powerful statement of Rabbi Chaim Vital:

> *A person's character traits are measured based upon how he is to his wife.*

According to Rabbi Chaim Vital, the barometer of character development is our behavior at home. *Chessed* not only begins at home; rather, the home is the ultimate arena for *chessed*. External deeds may be more reinforcing, but there are times when they must be sacrificed for an even greater ideal.

Performing good deeds while behaving inappropriately to one's family is like sitting in a Ferrari with a broken engine—impressive to others, but it won't get you far. Such a person is responding to emotions, not intellect. "Values informed by pure moods masquerade as benevolence."[10] Protecting ourselves from such a trap requires the awareness of both the emotions in the moment and our overarching

---

10   In Professor William Kolbrener's review essay of Rabbi Soloveitchik, he writes: "Values informed by pure moods only masquerade as benevolence, and are in fact mere self-serving projections, psychic mechanisms designed to cover up 'inner crisis.'" Found in William Kolbrener, "Into the Whirlwind: The Persistence of the Dialectic in the Works of Rabbi Joseph B. Soloveitchik," *Tradition*, 40:2, (2007): 90.

values. The very awareness of the emotional pull makes it less likely to take over, thereby allowing the intellect to honestly choose the proper present-moment behavior.

CLARIFYING THE MEANS AND ENDS

In *Pirkei Avos* (2:12), Rabbi Yossi states: "And all your actions should be for the sake of Heaven." Rabbi Simcha Bunim of Peshischa interprets the Mishnah by explaining that when you are behaving for the sake of Heaven, that itself should be done for the sake of Heaven.[11] The implication is that we can be pursuing a value in an inappropriate way. Valuable goals do not justify inappropriate means. We are not only evaluated based on "big accomplishments"; we are judged based on our everyday behaviors. What may appear as unimportant is actually the most essential. Life is not merely about striving to become an *eved Hashem* (servant of God); it is about acting as an *eved Hashem*.

When Rabbi Elchanan Wasserman eulogized his *rebbi*, the Chafetz Chaim, he explained that the Jewish definition of greatness can only be appreciated when the story of the private life is told. Usually, the more we enter the private life of someone, the more we recognize their flaws. With the Chafetz Chaim, the opposite was true. His outward greatness mirrored the way he treated those closest to him.[12]

Shmuel HaNavi chastised Shaul HaMelech: "To listen is better than a choice sacrifice; to pay attention is better than the fat of rams."[13] At times, we get so caught up in our sacrifices that we forget to listen and pay attention to what God really wants. In the introduction to

---

11 Rabbi Menachem Mendel of Kotzk states a similar idea about the verse, "*Tzedek tzedek tirdof*" (*Devarim* 16:20). Righteousness must be pursued with righteous means.

12 Rabbi Aharon Feldman, *The River, the Kettle, and the Bird: A Torah Guide to Successful Marriage* (Feldheim Publishers, 1987), p. 44.

13 *Shmuel I* 15:22.

Rabbi Chaim Ozer Grodzinski's *sefer*, *Achiezer*, he writes that the *sefer* was delayed many years because he was dealing with the needs of the community. The needs of the poor villager, the struggling couple, and the depressed adolescent took precedence over writing a *sefer* that would be studied by hundreds.[14] He recognized what was needed of him in the moment. He did not merely teach wisdom. He lived with wisdom.

T R Y :

1. Try to clarify what is truly important to you and why. Imagine you are ninety years old and reviewing your life. How do you want to have lived so that you can look back at your life and say, "I am happy with the way I lived my life"?

2. Research shows that those who set aside time to clarify their values are less apathetic, more critical in their thinking, and are more likely to follow through on decisions.[15]

3. Engage in a *mussar* pactice. *Mussar* can be understood as a time to (a) clarify your values; (b) become more aware of your personal inclinations, traits in need of improvement, and potential blind spots; and (c) think of practical changes that you would like to make and how to implement them. You may find it helpful to study from a text that assists in clarifying values and includes recommendations for behavioral change.

4. Throughout the day, try to take a minute or two to pause and ask yourself if you are living the way you want to live (see chapter 10, "Self-Regulation").

---

14   Initially heard from Rabbi Eytan Feiner.
15   Sidney B. Simon, Leland W. Howe, and Howard Kirschenbaum, *Values Clarification* (Grand Central Publishing, 2009), p. 12.

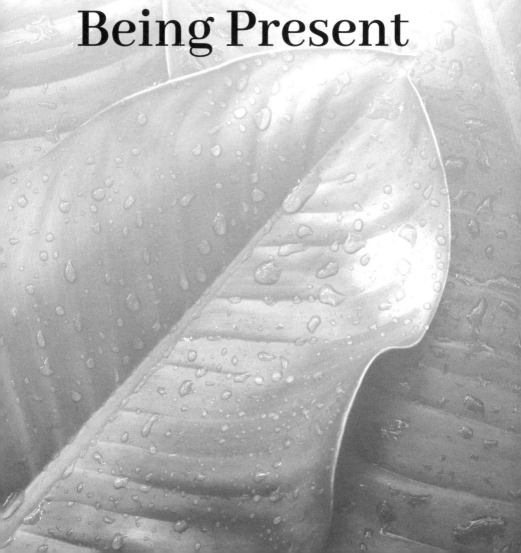

The Value of Being Present

Mindful Relationships

When Mom entered the living room and noticed her teenage son and his two friends preoccupied with their cell phones, she said, "It's a shame kids don't talk to each other anymore. When I was young, nobody even had cell phones." Her son responded, "Mom, we **were** talking to each other," and proceeded to show her the text messages they were sending one another.[1]

As the world is changing, so is the nature of communication. Cell phones can hurt people's attempts at interpersonal connection by just being in the room. In one study, pairs of strangers speaking to

---

1   There is halachic precedence for differentiating communicating in person and communicating via writing. There is a halachah that if you did not see someone you are close to in more than thirty days, you recite a blessing. The *Mishnah Berurah* (225:5) writes: "If you become close to someone through writing and then see the person, you do not say the blessing. Why? Because even though writing can bring people closer, the love is not nearly as great as seeing someone face to face." There are few adequate replacements for genuine human interaction.

each other reported lower closeness and relationship quality when their phones were readily accessible.[2]

The culprit isn't only cell phones. The cell phone is merely symbolic of the distracted mind that is focused on what we need to do next at the expense of the now. I was recently at a conference and struggled with mindfully speaking to the person in front me because I was thinking of all the other people I wanted to speak to. The anticipation for the future was at the expense of the present. Cultivating mindfulness helps us be more present to those in front of us. Mindfulness can be much more than a *self*-help technique; it can be used to care for others.

PAYING ATTENTION

The distracted mind makes it difficult to be emotionally present. What can we do?

One solution could be to limit external distractions, such as not looking at or answering a phone in the middle of a conversation. Alternatively, we can learn to raise the volume of the present. This can be accomplished by paying attention to our physical sensations and environment. The distractions may still be there, but they won't take up as much space. We can learn to look at our loved ones and truly notice them. We can be there for them, by "being" with them.

Near the end of his life, when Moshe Rabbeinu speaks to B'nei Yisrael, he talks about the covenant as applying to "whoever is here, standing with us today."[3] Rabbi Moshe Bogomilsky asks: If it already says, "whoever is here," why does it also need to say, "with us"? He explains that just because someone is physically present does not

---

2   Andrew K. Przybylski and Netta Weinstein, "Can you connect with me now? How the presence of mobile communication technology influences face-to-face conversation quality," *Journal of Social and Personal Relationships* 30, no. 3 (2013): 237–246.

3   *Devarim* 29:14.

mean they are truly present in mind and body.[4] When we are with another, we should strive to have our entire selves be with them.

In Dr. David Pelcovitz's eulogy for his father, Rabbi Raphael Pelcovitz, he noted that when his father spoke to others, he was able to hone in to what truly mattered to them. He recalled that his father would often say, "Attention must be paid."[5] Growing up in Rabbi Pelcovitz's shul, I was fortunate to have been a recipient of his mindful awareness of others. One of the last times I saw him was at a busy *kiddush*. Upon wishing him a good Shabbos, he proceeded to ask me about different aspects of my life. Although it was a noisy and crowded room, and there were others waiting to speak to him, in those few moments Rabbi Pelcovitz treated me as if I were the only person in the room. He knew how to be mindful of others. Attention was paid.

I AND THOU

To be mindful of others requires one to see beyond oneself.
To see beyond oneself requires a self.

Rabbi Avraham Yitzchak HaKohen Kook writes: "If there is no I, there is no you."[6] It is difficult to properly and sustainably care for another if one does not care for oneself.[7] Moreover, compassion of the self can increase compassion for others. When I am aware of what I feel, then I can better understand and feel for you. To see what it would be like to be you, I need to first understand what it's like to be me.

---

4   Rabbi Moshe Bogomilsky, *Vedibarta Bam: Devarim.*
5   A reference from Arthur Miller's play, *Death of a Salesman.*
6   *Orot Hakodesh* 3:3, p. 140.
7   Hillel said, "If I am here then all is here" (*Sukkah* 53a). I heard Rabbi Binyomin Eisenberger explain that Hillel is teaching us that we can only manage life's challenges when we have a sense of self.

I once saw my *rebbi* crying when he was saying *Tehillim* for a sick child. I knew that my *rebbi* did not know this specific child and I asked him how he was able to cry so intensely for someone he never met. He responded that whenever he prays for a sick child, he thinks about what it would be like if his own child were sick. He tried to see the world through the eyes of another.

PAIN AND LOVE

Sitting with the emotional experience of the one we care about is difficult because if we are truly empathic, then we too are in pain. Therefore, when another is expressing frustration, it is usually easier to engage in fixing mode. At times, this is what they need, but it often stems from a desire to decrease our own discomfort. Instead, we can join them in their pain and we can validate them. This may be emotionally draining, but it's usually more helpful.

Validation is more than agreeing with their words and providing platitudes like, "It's OK to feel that way." Truly sitting with someone expresses, "I'm here for you. It pains me to see you in this situation, but I'm willing to sit with you in discomfort because I care about you. I accept you with your strengths and blemishes. I accept you when you feel happy or sad. In this moment, you're OK just the way you are." To do this, we have to be aware of our own discomfort, and then make the decision to sit with it for the sake of a greater value: the value of being there for someone we care for. If love is putting someone else's needs before our own, then sincere validation is an act of love. My *rebbi* was willing to sit in pain as he cried for another. He was willing to love.

Several years ago, my brother was in the midst of a specific struggle for which he visited a number of different *rabbanim* for their guidance, blessings, and encouragement. He told me that the most impactful meeting was with a *rav* who hardly spoke. For almost forty minutes, the *rav* just sat there by his side, crying. The *rav* didn't just feel the initial pain; there was a continuous cry. He was willing to fully experience the pain of another. During that time, the *rav* did not respond to his phone or to a knock at the door. In that moment, my brother's pain was his pain. In that moment, my brother was not alone. That was the greatest comfort.

When we are faced with difficulty, we not only struggle with the problem itself; we struggle with the feelings of loneliness that ensue from the hardship. Having someone by our side who understands us cushions the pain from life's challenges.[8]

EQUANIMITY

Responding in an adaptive, compassionate manner requires equanimity. Equanimity entails noticing uncomfortable feelings and making space for them. It is holding emotions in awareness without letting them control behaviors.

For example, when someone upsets us, awareness of the anger actually makes it easier to manage it. Instead of becoming angry for feeling angry, we can validate ourselves. We can remind ourselves that we are allowed to feel—and we have little control of the immediate emotion. This is not an excuse for inappropriate behavior because we can still control the ensuing behavioral response.[9] Responding with anger is rarely appropriate.[10] It is also rarely effective. Rationalizing an angry response is tempting. It minimizes guilt and its ensuing discomfort. Yet, there is little justification for such rationalization. "The calm words of the wise are heard before the shouts of a ruler

---

8   For example, see Ian H. Stanley, Melanie A. Hom, Carol Chu, Sean P. Dougherty, Austin J. Gallyer, Sally Spencer-Thomas, Leah Shelef, et al., "Perceptions of belongingness and social support attenuate PTSD symptom severity among firefighters: A multi-study investigation," *Psychological Services* (2018).

9   It was discussed in chapter 1 that, in the moment, it is usually more effective to be compassionate of our initial emotional response. Still, we can work on specific processes that may limit future anger.

10   See *Mishneh Torah, Hilchos Dei'os* 2:3.

over fools" (*Koheles* 9:17). Sometimes, we assume we need to raise our voice to be heard, but this is not so. Words spoken softly are heard most clearly.[11]

When we observe anger with compassion, we are less consumed by it. When we are noticing our experience, we are less likely to respond on autopilot. We can act more rationally and less impulsively. Doing so increases peace—not just peace between I and thou, but peace within ourselves.

THINKING ABOUT THOU

Our default state breeds self-centeredness. We only know of the world through our own immediate experience.[12] It can be challenging to see the world from a different perspective.

> *Rabbi Avrohom Kamenetsky was once driving with his father, Reb Yaakov, on Coney Island Avenue in Brooklyn. As Reb Avrohom sat at a red light poised to jump out ahead of the adjacent bus for the one lane open ahead, he was surprised to hear his father tell him, "You must let the bus go first. A large group takes precedence over just two people."*[13]

The greatness in this story is not that Rabbi Yaakov Kamenetsky instructed his son to let the bus go first. Many of us would react to this anecdote by committing to follow in the path of Reb Yaakov and allow buses right of way in the future. Yet, we would be remiss if that is the only message we take from this story. Reb Yaakov's greatness

---

11   See also the Talmud in *Shabbos* (34a), which states that there are three things one should ask the members of his house on Erev Shabbos: "Have you tithed?" "Did you make an *eruv*?" and "Did you light the candles?" The Talmud explains that these should be asked with calmness so that they will be heard.

12   See Rabbi Mayer Twersky's essay, http://torahweb.org/torah/2000/parsha/rtwe_chay-eysara.html.

13   Yonason Rosenblum and Rabbi Noson Kamenetsky, *Reb Yaakov: The Life and Times of HaGaon Rabbi Yaakov Kamenetsky* (Mesorah Publications, 1993), p. 20.

was not simply in letting the bus go first. His greatness was that he thought about the people on the bus. He saw beyond himself.

Seeing the world through another's eyes requires pausing and make a conscious effort to understand where another may be coming from. I can remind myself that just like I struggle, he struggles. Just like I experience pain, he experiences pain. Because I am not you, I can never fully understand why you behave differently than I do. We should treat others with the same understanding and sensitivity we desire. Rabbi Akiva said, "Love your fellow like yourself; this is a fundamental principle in the Torah."[14] Pausing, thinking, and consciously choosing to see the bigger picture is a fundamental principle of the Torah.

BEAUTIFUL SOULS

In chapter 4, we discussed the importance of identifying with the *neshamah*—the part of ourselves that is pure. Let us add a point now: Just like it is important to recognize the beauty in ourselves, we must recognize the beauty in others. Just like you are a diamond, others are diamonds as well.

Identifying with the soul removes the barriers between us. The *Baal Hatanya* writes: "There can be no true love and fraternity between those who regard their bodies as primary and their souls as secondary."[15] On the physical level, we are separate. Therefore, it is not uncommon to enter a room and view the other as a potential competitor. But, on the level of soul, we are united; we all come from the same source. We are all on the same team striving toward a common goal of getting closer to our Father. Each person is someone from whom I can learn and toward whom I can be kind.

---

14 *Yerushalmi, Nedarim* 9:4.
15 *Tanya*, chap. 32.

When Rabbi Yisrael Salanter was on his deathbed, the Jewish community assigned a watchman to stay with him. On the night that Reb Yisrael sensed was his last, the watchman was frightened, afraid to be alone in a room with a dead body. A teacher of introspection and repentance, we may imagine Reb Yisrael would have liked to spend his last moments reviewing his life and repenting. Perhaps this is what he did, inwardly. Outwardly, he practiced what he preached: personal spirituality should not take precedence over the needs of another human being. And so, Reb Yisrael spent the last moments of his life soothing the watchman.[16]

Rabbi Yisrael Salanter spent his last few moments in this world comforting another human being. He recognized what was needed of him in the moment; indeed, those precious moments were very spiritual. As the Torah states: *"V'ahavta l'rei'acha kamocha, ani Hashem*—And you should love your neighbor as yourself, I am Hashem."[17] When I love my brother like myself, God is present. When God is present and I am connected to spirituality, I can love my brother like myself.[18]

T R Y :

1. The next time you are with someone, try to notice your breath, notice how your body is feeling, and notice where your mind is going. Then, try to pay attention to this person's face. Notice their skin, notice the tone of their voice,

---

16 Adapted from Hillel Goldberg, *The Fire Within: The Living Heritage of the Mussar Movement* (Mesorah Publications, 1987), p. 59.

17 *Vayikra* 19:18.

18 The Talmud in *Bava Basra*, 99a, explains that when B'nei Yisrael was doing the will of God, the *Keruvim* were facing each other. When God is present, we can properly face another.

notice their eyes. Try to imagine what it's like to be them in this moment. Try to ask yourself: *How can I respond in a way that will be helpful for this person?*

2. As you are listening to another, notice how often you are thinking about how you want to respond. See if you can put that on hold and truly be with the other. See if you can wait a few moments before responding. Pausing before responding increases the likelihood of the speaker feeling heard and understood.

3. When you respond to another, try to ask yourself: Do I say what makes me sound wise, or do I say what the person needs to hear?

4. Notice your breath and your body. Try to think of someone with whom you are having a difficult time. Try to ask yourself why that person may be behaving the way they do. Try to understand what circumstances in their life may have led them to act in such a way. Think of what pain they may be going through in their life. Most of the time when people are acting inappropriately, it is their way of dealing with pain. Thinking of another's pain increases compassion and tolerance.

CHAPTER 8

Patience and Tolerance

Hurriedness leads to regret.[1]

Rabbi Chaim Vital

The advent of Google and smartphones has enabled us to obtain immediate answers to almost any question that passes through the mind. We no longer need to wait until we find a dictionary, encyclopedia, or person to answer our questions. We no longer need to wait until the stores are open to purchase an item. In our modern age, it is becoming increasingly difficult to cultivate patience.

Behaving impulsively has consequences. It leads to difficulties in relationships, creates inner stress, and increases the possibility of making poor decisions. Slowing down requires effort, yet the rewards

---

1   *Shaarei Kedushah* 1:6.

are worth it. As the Alter of Kelm writes: "*Savlanus* (patience) is the source of all positive traits."[2]

Psychological studies demonstrate that when people are rushing, they are less likely to properly care for others—even if they are rushing to give a lecture on the importance of helping others![3] Rushing reduces our ability to be aware of the consequences of our actions and to act according to our values.

This idea is demonstrated in the following Talmudic statement:

> *Taking long steps takes away 1/500 of eyesight. How do you restore it? By drinking the Friday night Kiddush.*[4]

Long steps—in other words, rushing—hinder the ability to properly see. Rushing hinders perspective. What is the solution? The Friday night Kiddush. Sanctifying Shabbos and dedicating a day to being mindful restores the reflective capability.

Slowing down helps us become more aware of ourselves and our values. This explains why patience does not conflict with the valuable trait of *zerizus*, alacrity. Alacrity is not merely acting quickly; it is acting with clarity. Behaving quickly in itself is not considered praiseworthy. In fact, this often stems from laziness. As Rabbi Menachem Mendel of Kotzk writes:

> *The patient (masun) person is the one who acts with yishuv ha'daas (a settled mind) and doesn't hurry things. The lazy*

---

2   *Chochmah U'Mussar*, vol. 1, p. 432 (found in *Alei Shur*, vol. 2, p. 214).

3   See the Darley and Batson study mentioned in the Foreword.

4   *Berachos* 43b.

person does the opposite. He is too lazy to settle himself and therefore acts impulsively.[5]

The lazy person doesn't put in the effort to slow down and act judiciously. In contrast, the patient person's effort to slow down enables him to gain clarity. Clarity leads to alacrity. Behaving patiently helps us to be more aware of what is important and how to behave; hence, we will be swift in acting correctly.[6]

TOLERANCE

Mindfulness isn't necessarily about feeling better (at least not the way we are understanding it). Mindfulness is the willingness to *carry* discomfort for the sake of something greater. This is the essence of *savlanus*, which means both "patience" and "tolerance." Rabbi Shlomo Wolbe explains that the root of the word is *saval*, which means to "bear" or to "carry." *Savlanus* requires the willingness to bear discomfort.[7] Usually, the closer someone is to us, the greater the need for *savlanus*. In fact, in Hebrew, marrying a woman is referred to as *"nosei ishah*—carrying a wife." Maintaining a healthy relationship requires tolerating your spouse. This tolerance doesn't entail ignoring your emotions; rather, *savlanus* is recognizing and validating your emotions and not allowing them to negatively affect your actions.

Rabbi Wolbe advises setting aside time daily to work on this trait. There is a value in setting aside time to tolerate what is taking place, to accepting the current reality. Accepting reality includes recognizing our limitations in changing those who are close to us.

---

5   *Emes V'Emunah* 38.

6   As Rabbi Pinchas ben Yair states: *"Zehirus* (watchfulness) leads to *zerizus* (alacrity)" (*Avodah Zarah* 20b).

7   See Rabbi Shlomo Wolbe, *Alei Shur*, vol. 2, p. 214. Most of this paragraph is based on Rabbi Wolbe's teachings on this topic.

PATIENCE WITH YOURSELF

Savlanus is not just for others; it is for ourselves as well. Many people have a natural drive to move forward as quickly as possible—both in the physical and spiritual realms. Such a drive requires caution, because at times, it can even lead to anger. As Shlomo HaMelech writes:

> *The foolishness of man perverts his way, and his heart is angered at God.*[8]

In his commentary on this verse, the Vilna Gaon explains that sometimes a person gives up serving God because it appears too difficult. But his frustration stems from foolishness. He was trying to do too much too fast, yet this was unsustainable and could not succeed. If something is truly too difficult, it may not be what is currently expected from us. As we say in our prayers: *"L'svunaso ein mispar*—His understanding has no end."[9] God is more understanding than we sometimes give Him credit for.

Successful growth usually occurs slowly, step by step. It requires patience. You can't rush the caterpillar into becoming a butterfly. That which is fast usually does not last.[10]

THE FEAR OF SLOWING DOWN

For many, slowing down is difficult due to the fear of not accomplishing:

- Some fear that if they study slowly, they won't become wise.

---

8   *Mishlei* 19:13.

9   *Tehillim* 147:5; the common interpretation for this verse is that His understanding is beyond comprehension.

10   Research shows that people are more likely to demonstrate a statement as truthful when it rhymes. See Matthew S. McGlone and Jessica Tofighbakhsh, "Birds of a feather flock conjointly (?): Rhyme as reason in aphorisms," *Psychological Science* 11, no. 5 (2000): 424–428.

- Others fear that if they don't use every moment of work efficiently, they won't make enough money to support their family.

Such thinking can be detrimental. In many situations, maximizing every moment actually *reduces* efficiency and the net gain is less. Additionally, the person working at maximum capacity will require more breaks, will need vacations sooner, and the quality of the work may be diminished. Sometimes, working less is actually working more.

The desire to stay perpetually busy can have other negative side effects. In the desire to feel accomplished, one may waste time on trivial matters with the illusion that they are actually doing something productive. For example, a patient described that before purchasing a pair of socks online, he spent over an hour reading about the different materials that socks are made of and researching where he could find them for the best price. Although this story may seem abnormal, wasting time with inessential matters is quite common and at times tempting; it distracts us from real life.

In contrast, when we are more conscious of what we are doing, we can accomplish more. When we slow down, we get further.

THE HOLINESS IN NOW

Waiting may be difficult because we think there is something more important that we need to achieve. However, in reminding ourselves of what life is truly about, we can find meaning in the now. In God's initial conversation with Moshe Rabbeinu, He says, "The ground that you are standing on is holy."[11] The Chafetz Chaim explains that God was telling Moshe that the potential for holiness lies in this specific moment, in this specific situation. Any given moment is an opportunity to reach closer to God.

---

11   *Shemos* 3:5.

> *After the death of Rabbi Moshe of Kobryn, the Kotzker*
> *Rebbe asked one of his students, "What was most import-*
> *ant to your teacher?" The disciple thought and then replied,*
> *"Whatever he was doing at the moment."*[12]

He found meaning in the present, not in the contemplation of future accomplishment. If we are distracted from the present moment, we are distracted from life itself. Greatness is not found in some distant future. It can be found right now.

T R Y :

1. Eating can be an opportunity to work on improving patience (and health). Try to eat slowly and mindfully. When you are eating, try to wait until you swallow your first bite before you put in the next. (Note: This may not be recommended if you are someone who is already overly conscious of eating.)

2. Remind yourself how the mind often magnifies the negative consequences of waiting. Recognizing this probably won't take away the feeling—the point is to encourage yourself not to respond to it.

3. Think of something that is frustrating you about someone you are close to. Notice what shows up. Notice where you feel it in the body and what your mind is saying about it. When we are more mindful of our thoughts, we are more likely to recognize what is truly troubling us (sometimes, we may even be ashamed where the mind is going; but if we can't be aware of it, we cannot manage it). Upon noticing what's bothering you, think of what is important to you and clarify what may be the healthiest way to deal with this person.

---

12   Martin Buber, *Tales of the Hasidim* (Schocken Books Inc, 1991), p. 173.

Upon clarifying how you want to behave, see if you can be willing to make space for the discomfort. Finding meaning in the discomfort can make it more bearable.

4. Consider studying the *Tomer Devorah* by Rabbi Moshe Cordovero; it is a helpful guide for improving tolerance. Rabbi Cordovero explains how we are charged with emulating God by responding to others with the same acceptance, compassion, and love that He showers upon us.

5. Try to use different situations as opportunities for cultivating patience, such as when sitting in traffic, waiting on line, or waiting for food to be served.

> *It is told that the Gerrer Rebbe, the Imrei Emes, was once sitting and waiting to be served dinner. The Rebbetzin had been delayed and the Rebbe was kept waiting. One of the chassidim, reflecting upon the Rebbe's anticipated displeasure with the waste of time, asked, "Rebbe, what do we learn now?" The Rebbe replied, "Now, we learn savlanus."*[13]

---

13   From Rabbi Binyomin Forst's chapter in *Step by Step* (Shaar Press, 2012), "Tolerance."

CHAPTER 9

FOMO and Contentment

> The meager present is superior to
> and more valuable than the most
> promising future.[1]
>
> The Alter of Novarodok

A s I write this, I am missing out on many opportunities. It is a beautiful day outside. I could be swimming, I could be spending time with my kids, or I could be vacationing somewhere. Then again, if I was doing any one of those things, I would still be missing out on something else.

We are always missing out on something. The fear of missing out (FOMO for short) is a hindrance to finding peace in the moment. Not surprisingly, in correlational studies, those with higher scores on the

---

1   *Madreigas Ha'adam*, *"Tikkun Hamiddos"*; translation from Meir Levin, *Novarodok: A Movement That Lived in Struggle and Its Unique Approach to the Problem of Man* (Jason Aronson, Inc., 1996), p. 126.

Fear of Missing Out scale have greater use of social media and lower levels of life satisfaction.[2] FOMO leads to missing out on the present.

Running away from the present to chase that which is outside of us can lead to trouble.[3] When we are not at peace in the now, we may seek comfort with inappropriate distractions. Once we are engaged in the pursuit of external and immediate pleasures, there is no end—we are constantly chasing the next high. As Rabbi Chaim Friedlander writes: "Not being at peace with oneself in this moment is both a cause and a result of bad deeds." Reminding ourselves that we have what we need in this moment and that we can be fulfilling our purpose in this moment can lead to a serenity that will prevent us from seeking distraction elsewhere. A full cup stays steady. The empty cup will easily fly from one place to another. When we are at peace, we don't need to move.

LACK OF PRESENCE

In addition to the concern of physically running away from the present, there is also the challenge of not being mentally present. At work, a person may be thinking of vacation. When vacationing, he may be thinking of work. The mind's nature is to be thinking of the next experience. A patient described that during the Shabbos morning prayers, he was thinking of the delicious meal that would follow. He then rushed through the meal so he could have more time for a nap—and, ironically, he noted that he was napping so he could be more alert for learning and prayer.

Most of us are challenged by this in some form. We can be overly focused on what's next at the expense of the now. However, by

---

2   Andrew Przybylski, Kou Murayama, Cody R. DeHaan, and Valerie Gladwell, "Motivational, emotional, and behavioral correlates of fear of missing out," *Computers in Human Behavior* 29, no. 4 (2013): 1841–1848.

3   Most of this paragraph is based on Rabbi Chaim Friedlander's *Sifsei Chaim*, "Middos V'Avodas Hashem," vol. 2, p. 37.

recognizing that the mind is constantly going to the next activity and reminding ourselves of the circular nature of such thinking, we can bring our attention back to the present moment. This is why mindfulness is intertwined with values. If there is little purpose in what I am doing, I should pay attention elsewhere. But if I am living according to my values in this very moment, there is nothing else. Now is where it's at.

CHASING EXPERIENCE

FOMO is based on a faulty—yet powerful—premise. It is based on the idea that there is something more exciting than the present, that there is an external experience that we are missing out on. Society convinces us that obtaining a plethora of experiences has value in itself. In discussing different myths adapted by the modern world, Yuval Harari writes:

> *Romanticism tells us that in order to make the most of our human potential we must have as many different experiences as we can. We must open ourselves to a wide spectrum of emotion; we must sample various kinds of relationships; we must try different cuisines; we must learn to appreciate different styles of music...We hear again and again the romantic myths about "how a new experience opened my eyes and changed my life."*[4]

The more we believe in this myth, the more we feel lacking from the pleasures we have not yet experienced. Granted, positive experiences are important. In fact, there is research that positive experiences are correlated with happiness.[5] But if that is a goal in itself, we will feel

---

4   Yuval Noah Harari, *Sapiens: A Brief History of Humankind* (Random House, 2014), p. 115.
5   Amit Bhattacharjee and Cassie Mogilner, "Happiness from ordinary and extraordinary experiences," *Journal of Consumer Research* 41, no. 1 (2013): 1–17. Interestingly, as

incomplete because there will always be some experiences we are missing. Moreover, the yearning for the next experience will prevent us from experiencing the greatest experience of all: the experience of meaningfully living in the present.

FEAR OF THE WRONG CHOICE

For some, FOMO is more than just missing experiences; it is the fear that one has made the wrong decision. The Latin root of the word "decision" means to cut off: every decision excludes alternatives. Every time we move toward something, we are also moving away from something. Ideally, we want to always make the perfect decisions, but this is impossible. Trying to constantly make perfect decisions can lead to paralysis by analysis. It is healthier to make a suboptimal decision than to remain indecisive or to vacillate from one option to another.[6]

Since we are imperfect, we are going to make mistakes. We will make decisions that will lead to missing out. There is no other way. Only God is perfect. Instead of berating ourselves for every mistake that leads to a failed opportunity, we can remind ourselves that this comes with the human condition. Instead of fighting it, we can flow with it. It is less emotionally draining, we'll be easier to deal with, and it will be easier to maximize and appreciate the now. We can learn to focus on what is, not what could be.

Being present can be difficult. There can be this nagging feeling that we should be doing something different. For some, it is the feeling of wanting to be someone else. We should be careful in chasing

---

people age, they are more likely to find happiness in ordinary experiences. Perhaps it is because they realize that the ordinary is truly extraordinary.

6   Part of this paragraph is based on the chapter, "Focus on Resistance to Decision," in Irvin D. Yalom, *The Gift of Therapy* (Harper Perennial, 2002), pp. 148–149.

these illusions. Life is not out there. Life is right here, right now. Peace can be found in this moment.

T R Y :

1. Spend a few moments reflecting on previous experiences that you were looking forward to. Did they meet your expectations? Did they make you as happy as you thought they would?
2. What are your happiest memories? Are they moments of physical pleasures or moments with meaning?
3. Reflect on the following anonymous quote:

    > *First, I was dying to finish high school. Then, I was dying to finish college. After that, I was dying to get married. Then, I was dying to have children. Then, I was dying for the kids to get older so I could marry them off and relax. After that, I was dying to retire. Now, I'm just dying, and I realize that I never really lived.*

    Although we need to appropriately plan for the future, we should be careful not to become overly focused on the future at the expense of meaningfully living in the present.

CHAPTER 10

Self-Regulation

The primary obligation of man is to constantly engage in refining his character.[1]

Vilna Gaon

A psychologist once noted that if people can learn to be present, make space for uncomfortable thoughts and feelings, and live according to their values, then psychologists would be out of business.[2] Most self-improvement is dependent on these three processes.

BEING PRESENT

Someone interviewing Jon Kabat-Zinn (the founder of MBSR) asked him what he thought about multitasking. He replied, "Toxic." Although it may sound extreme, his response affected me. It helped

---

1 *Even Sheleimah* 1:2.
2 I heard similar comments by both Steven Hayes and Kirk Strosahl, cofounders of Acceptance and Commitment Therapy (ACT).

me become more aware of the dangers of multitasking. Multitasking is harmful for the brain,[3] and it reduces overall efficiency. There is halachic precedence for this. *Tosafos* explains that we should not mix two joyous occasions nor combine different mitzvos together because we should be focusing on one task at a time.[4] We should be focusing on the task in front of us.

A few days ago, a patient was describing how she was driving while simultaneously speaking to someone on the phone and drinking coffee. Not only was she increasing the risk of an accident,[5] she wasn't able to fully attend to the conversation. (She also probably didn't appreciate the coffee too much.) Running on autopilot has consequences. To behave properly, we need to pause and be present.

MAKING SPACE FOR EMOTIONS

Pausing is not enough. We can pause and still make a conscious decision to continue with unhealthy behaviors because we don't want to stay with the present moment. We either want to experience a greater pleasure, or we want to run away from current discomfort. Not giving in to unhealthy pleasures requires sitting with emotions in the present moment. While some propose that mindfulness helps by decreasing the intensity of emotions, most researchers report[6]

---

3   Kep Kee Loh, and Ryota Kanai, "Higher Media Multi-Tasking Activity Is Associated with Smaller Gray-Matter Density in the Anterior Cingulate Cortex," *Plos One* 9, no. 9 (2014).

4   *Mo'ed Katan* 8b.

5   Gemma F. Briggs, Graham J. Hole, and Jim AJ Turner, "The impact of attentional set and situation awareness on dual tasking driving performance," *Transportation Research Part F: Traffic Psychology and Behaviour* (2017); and Michael L. Alosco, et al., "Both texting and eating are associated with impaired simulated driving performance," *Traffic Injury Prevention* 13.5 (2012): 468–475.

6   Rimma Teper, Zindel V. Segal, and Michael Inzlicht, "Inside the Mindful Mind: How Mindfulness Enhances Emotion Regulation Through Improvements in Executive Control," *Current Directions in Psychological Science* 22.6 (2013): 449–454.

that the primary benefit is the ability to be aware of our emotions and make space for them.[7]

Validation

If there are simple and effective ways to eliminate pain, we should utilize them, but merely suppressing emotions is not very effective.[8] There was a study conducted at the University of Washington[9] where sixty students were asked to solve mental arithmetic problems (a commonly used procedure to stimulate stress) in a short period of time. Upon completing the problems:

- Half the students were given a validating response. For example, they were told: "Completing math problems without a pencil or paper is frustrating. Most other participants have expressed the exact same feeling. I too would be upset if I were completing the task."
- The other half were given an invalidating response such as, "I don't understand why you feel that way. There's no need to get upset. Others were a little frustrated, but not as much as you seem to be."

Not surprisingly, the group that received the invalidating response had higher levels of negative affect as measured by self-report measures and higher heart rate and skin conductance levels (a physiological measure of stress) than the group that was validated.[10] Telling ourselves (and others), "We shouldn't feel that way," will make us feel worse. Reminding ourselves that it is OK to feel pacifies the emotion.

---

7   See *Rashi, Bamidbar* 21:4, *"Va'tikzar nefesh ha'am ba'derech,"* that B'nei Yisrael sinned because they did not have the space to contain the discomfort.

8   Campbell-Sills et. al, "Effects of suppression and acceptance on emotional responses of individuals with anxiety and mood disorders," 1251–1263.

9   Chad E. Shenk and Alan E. Fruzzetti, "The impact of validating and invalidating responses on emotional reactivity," *Journal of Social and Clinical Psychology* 30, no. 2 (2011): 163–183.

10 See *Tiferes Yisrael* commentary on *Avos* 4:18.

Healthy validation of emotions does not justify inappropriate behavior nor does it lend validity to the content of the thoughts related to the emotion. Rather, it is about allowing ourselves to observe and make space for experience.

Experiential Acceptance

Some try to avoid emotions by avoiding certain experiences:

- The person who doesn't want to feel the pain of loss or rejection avoids connection.
- The person who doesn't want to experience failure doesn't try.

Making space for fear, doubt, and hurt can free us. We don't need to live in a minefield with the constant fear of emotional devastation. Emotions don't destroy. Instead of trying to directly control emotions, we can learn not to be controlled by them.

There is a faulty assumption that we need to feel good to live good. It's like saying that we cannot jump into a cold pool until we have the right mindset. If that's the case, we'll be waiting at the pool edge for a long time. Instead, we can just jump in. We don't need to wait until we feel right. We can act the way we truly want, even if the feelings are not yet there.

When Yaakov Avinu was about to encounter his brother, Eisav, the Torah states that Yaakov was afraid. The *Abarbanel* explains that Yaakov's emotional response was normal—it did not demonstrate a lack of faith. Any healthy individual going to war is going to experience the psycho-physiological reaction of fear. The brave soldier is the one who feels the fear but marches on. Yaakov's faith was manifest in his willingness to continue on his journey despite his insecurity. The more we can make space for painful emotions, the less we will be held back by them. "*L'fum tzaara agra*—According to the pain is the reward."[11] Reward is dependent on our willingness to

---

11   *Avos* 5:23.

experience discomfort. The greater our capacity to feel, the greater our ability to grow.

LIVING ACCORDING TO ONE'S VALUES

Rabbi Avraham ben HaRambam writes: "He who appreciates the value of his goal will disregard any sacrifices needed to reach it."[12] If we can recognize the value of our goals, we will be more willing to experience the emotional discomfort necessary to achieve these goals.[13]

There is a popular psychology study known as the "Stanford marshmallow experiment." In this experiment, children were given the option to eat one marshmallow right away or wait fifteen minutes for two marshmallows. When the children were studied again later in life, those who had waited for two marshmallows were more likely to have better relationships, higher test scores, healthier body mass index, and better outcomes on different life measures.[14] So much of our success is dependent on whether we do what is easier in the moment or what is better for us in the long term. Are we willing to sacrifice the one marshmallow to eventually obtain two marshmallows? Are we willing to sacrifice temporary pleasure for long-term gain?

The marshmallow experiment parallels a beautiful *Midrash Tanchuma* that expounds the verse, "Behold, I set before you this day a blessing and a curse."[15] The midrash gives the following parable:

---

12 Rabbi Avraham ben HaRambam, *Sefer Hamaspik L'Ovdei Hashem*, *"Perishus"* (Abstinence).

13 The following example emphasizes this: If one were to stick a needle in you, you would be in pain. However, if it was explained that the needle was an injection that could save your life, it would still hurt, but it would be a different type of pain; it would be more tolerable. As Victor Frankl states in *Man's Search for Meaning* (Boston: Beacon Press Books, 1992), p. 117: "In some ways, suffering ceases to be suffering at the moment it finds a meaning."

14 Yuichi Shoda, Walter Mischel, and Philip K. Peake, "Predicting adolescent cognitive and self-regulatory competencies from preschool delay of gratification: Identifying diagnostic conditions," *Developmental Psychology* 26, no. 6 (1990): 978.

15 *Devarim* 11:26.

There is an elderly man sitting at a crossroads. One road has thorns and is then smooth, the other is initially smooth, but then has thorns. The elderly man guides the travelers to go down the thorny road, explaining that although it is initially thorny, it will eventually be smooth. Any wise person will listen to this man and go down that road. Those who don't will eventually stumble.[16]

There are many life situations in which the path that is initially easier will eventually be more difficult. Although we know this intellectually, we may still find ourselves going down that path. This usually occurs for one of two reasons. We either fail to fully appreciate the value of the long-term gain, or we recognize the value but simply succumb to impulse. The following image demonstrates this challenge:

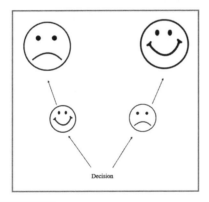

---

16   In Rabbi Paysach Krohn's *In the Spirit of the Maggid* (ArtScroll, 2008), p. 304, he quotes Rabbi Yaron Halbertal as saying that the above midrash is alluded to in *Mishlei* 19:21: "There are many thoughts in man's heart, but the advice of God will stand—*takum*." The word *takum* is an acronym for "*techilasah kotzim v'sofo meishor*—the beginning is full of thorns and the end is smooth." This can be interpreted one of two ways: (1) God's advice is to choose the path that is initially difficult and afterward pleasant, or (2) The path of serving God is initially difficult and afterward pleasant. According to the first understanding, the difficulty may only be in perception, yet upon actually following that path, it is not as difficult as it appeared. According to the second interpretation, the beginning of the path is experientially difficult.

In the moment of choice, do we do what is temporarily easier or what will be better in the long term? Do we go down the road that is initially smooth but eventually rough (left) or the road that is initially rough but eventually smooth (right). Ideally, most people would like both smiley faces, but this is rarely possible. Most valuable goals require effort. To help choose the right path, we can try to be BOLD:[17]

B—Breathe: Breathe slowly; slow down.

O—Observe: Observe what we are doing, feeling, thinking; be mindful.

L—Listen to values: Right now, what kind of person do we want to be? What path do we really want to travel down?

D—Decide on actions and do them: Choose actions that reflect our values.

This is mindfulness in the moment. It can help us slow down and redirect in a way that is more consistent with our values.

In his conclusion to *Koheles*, Shlomo HaMelech writes: "In the end, [after] everything has been heard, fear God and do His commandments, for this is the entirety of man."[18] Perhaps we can read the verse as follows:

1. We should be present and *hear*—hear ourselves, understand ourselves—pay attention to the present.

2. *Fear God* and recognize Him in our lives; remind ourselves of values.

3. Do His *mitzvos*. It is not enough to recognize intellectually; we should follow through with committed action toward values.

This is living boldly. This is the entirety of man.

---

17   This is from the Choice Point Model by Ann Bailey, Joseph Ciarrochi, and Russ Harris, *The Weight Escape: How to Stop Dieting and Start Living* (Shambhala Publications, 2014).

18   *Koheles* 12:13.

T R Y :

1. Ask God for help. The *Ramchal* writes at the end of the chapter on *zehirus* (watchfulness) that one cannot conquer evil without Divine assistance.

2. Try to dedicate time to learn Torah. The *Ramchal* writes that *limud haTorah* (Torah learning) brings a person to *zehirus*. Learning Torah, when studied properly and with the right intentions, has the ability to refine a person. "God created the *yetzer hara* and He created the Torah as its antidote" (*Kiddushin* 30b). Rabbeinu Bachya ibn Pakuda writes that the Torah strengthens, purifies, and illuminates the mind. It pulls man away from the foolishness that prevents man from seeing things the way they truly are.

3. Set aside time to clarify what is truly important to you and how you want to behave; commit to being mindful of your values.

4. In moments of choice, try to be BOLD. Take ten seconds to breathe, observe, listen, and decide.

CHAPTER 11

Can You Be Too Mindful?

The Torah was not given to angels.

Yoma 30a

O ne of the dangers with the written word is that it cannot be tailored for the individual.[1] Because we are each created differently, each one of us will require a different path toward self-improvement. It is a process that cannot be prescribed. Self-improvement requires us to be aware of ourselves—aware of our nature and aware of what will help us grow. In many cases, a good teacher or friend is invaluable in helping us become more aware of potential blind spots.

Awareness of ourselves entails recognizing when we are becoming too extreme in a given matter. Even mindfulness—like most things in life—can be taken to the extreme. There are some individuals whose nature is to try too hard to be mindful of themselves, others,

---

1 See the introduction to the *Tanya*, which describes how reading words of guidance from a book is not nearly as powerful as hearing them from a teacher, because the written word cannot be fully tailored toward the individual.

and of God. Emphasizing the importance of mindfulness to such people may hurt more than help. Such individuals will require a different message in order to achieve a healthy balance. As the *Rambam* explains, if one's nature is at one extreme, he should practice behaving in the opposite manner.[2] For example, one whose nature is to be overly lax should be encouraged to try harder. One whose nature it to be overly harsh and to push too hard and too fast should be encouraged to take things more lightly. Our task, the *Rambam* describes, is to move closer to the healthy median.

This idea is demonstrated by the Yerkes-Dodson Law.

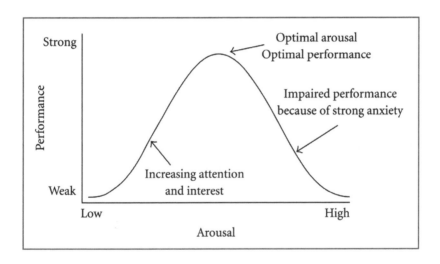

This law, described by psychologists Robert Yerkes and John Dillingham Dodson, demonstrates that increased arousal leads to an increase in performance. But only up to a point. At a certain level, too

---

2   *Mishneh Torah, Hilchos Dei'os*, chaps. 1 and 2.

much arousal decreases performance. For example, some students may perform worse if they aim for a grade of a hundred than if they were to aim for a ninety. The pressure to obtain the perfect grade may diminish performance. While those on the left side of the chart will need to try harder to improve performance, those on the right side should try less. Being cognizant of where we are will help us know how to get closer to the median.

A number of years ago, I was considering accepting upon myself a specific halachic stringency. Before doing so, I spoke to my *rebbi*,[3] who, instead of telling me what to do, gave a parable:

> *In a war, each side has a limited number of soldiers, and the general decides how to divide them. He can place the soldiers equally in different battles, or he can concentrate them in the important battles. The latter choice will increase the chances of winning the war.*

My *rebbi* explained that we only have a certain amount of emotional energy, and we have to decide how to divide it. If a halachic stringency does not take up much energy, there is probably little harm in accepting it. However, if it will be pulling emotional energy away from more important battles, it may be preferable to put in on hold. Recognizing our strengths and limitations helps us maintain a healthy balance.

In trying to achieve a healthy balance, it is helpful to remember that there is no perfect balance. We are rarely going to be at the peak of the curve. In life, we try to stay close to the middle without veering too far in any one direction. The key is to notice when we're tilting too far to any given direction and to gently pull ourselves back closer to the median. What worked yesterday may not work today; what is

---

3   Rabbi Moshe Stav.

right today may be wrong tomorrow. As the Alter of Slabodka said, "A thing and its opposite—contradictions—these are among the ways of God Himself."[4]

---

4 See Hillel Goldberg, *Between Berlin and Slobodka: Jewish Transition Figures from Eastern Europe* (KTAV Publishing House, 1989).

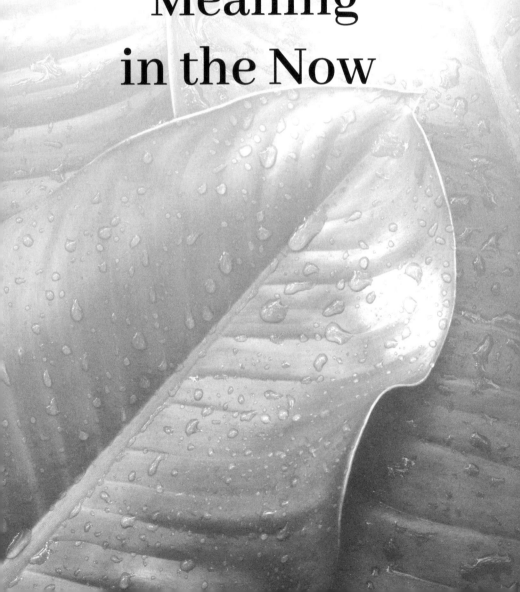

PART III

Meaning in the Now

CHAPTER 12

Mindful of God's World

A respectable guest was invited to eat in the home of a wealthy family. To honor the guest, the family bought a rare species of fish that was prepared exclusively for the visitor. Informed of the distinctiveness of this delicacy, the guest savored every bite. When asked by the host what he thought of the dish, he responded enthusiastically about its splendid flavor, saying it was one of the most delicious foods he had tasted. A few minutes later, the chef ran into the room stating that he accidentally served the honorable guest a regular piece of fish. Someone else had eaten the delicacy.[1]

Although the guest had eaten a regular piece of fish, it tasted extraordinary. Seeing as it was a regular piece of fish, it was not the specific taste of the fish that made it delicious—it was *how* he tasted it. He ate mindfully.

---

1 This story is adapted from John D. Teasdale and Zindel V. Segal, *The Mindful Way through Depression* (Guilford Press, 2007), p. 53.

We live in a beautiful world, yet we are often moving too fast to appreciate it. Slowing down and being mindful helps us see the extraordinary in the ordinary. It helps us appreciate the present. The more we appreciate the present, the less we need to run away from it.

There are two primary ways being mindful of the world can be used to serve God:

- We can view it as an exercise that research has shown to be beneficial for one's overall well-being. This is valuable either because of the requirement to maintain a healthy body[2] or because it can put us in a better state to observe other mitzvos. This is manifest in the *Rambam's* recommendation to enjoy nature as an antidote to melancholy. He writes:

  > *If one suffers from melancholy, he could treat it by listening to music, strolling among gardens and pretty buildings, or by looking at beautiful works of art and similar things to ease his spirit, and the melancholy will go away.*[3] *The intention in all this should be to maintain a healthy body. The purpose of a healthy body is to learn.*[4]

- Being mindful of eating and of nature can be viewed as a holy activity in itself. It can be a way to connect to the Divine. "It is a high level to eat in order to learn; but it is even higher to learn in order to know how to eat."[5] Being mindful of God's

---

2   There are a variety of opinions regarding the source and extent of this requirement. See *Berachos* 32b and *Maharsha*; *Mishneh Torah, Hilchos Rotzei'ach U'Shemiras Nefesh* 11:4–5, and *Minchas Chinuch*; see also *Tur Shulchan Aruch, Orach Chaim* 155.

3   This is based on the Talmud (*Berachos* 57b), where it says: "Three things calm a person: listening to music, pleasant scenery, and a pleasant aroma."

4   *Shemoneh Perakim*, chap. 5.

5   Adapted from Moshe Mykoff, *The Empty Chair: Finding Hope and Joy—Timeless Wisdom from a Hasidic Master, Rebbe Nachman of Breslov* (Jewish Lights, 1996).

world can be a religious act in itself. It can also be used to increase love and fear of God. As the *Rambam* writes:

What is the path [to attain] love and fear of God? When a person contemplates His wondrous and great deeds and creations and appreciates His infinite wisdom that surpasses all comparison, he will immediately love, praise, and glorify [Him], yearning with tremendous desire to know [God's] great name, as David stated, "My soul thirsts for the Lord, for the living God."⁶ When he [continues] to reflect on these same matters, he will immediately recoil in awe and fear, appreciating how he is a tiny, lowly, and dark creature, standing with his flimsy, limited wisdom before He who is of perfect knowledge...⁷

According to the *Rambam*, being aware of and paying attention to one's surroundings will lead to a heightened love and fear of God.⁸ It is not merely a tool to enhance specific mitzvos; mindfulness can be a path to connecting to the Divine. Still, according to the *Rambam*, merely seeing nature does not suffice; there must be a purposeful intention, a contemplation of the Divine within nature. Attention sets the stage for intention.

---

6   *Tehillim* 42:3.

7   *Mishneh Torah, Hilchos Yesodei HaTorah* 2:2. Translations of the *Rambam* have been adapted from Eliyahu Touger, *Mishneh Torah* (Moznaim Publishing Corporation, 1989).

8   Interestingly, Rabbi Ahron Soloveichik explains that the *"maasav u'v'ruaav ha'nifla'im*—His wondrous great deeds and creations," mentioned by the *Rambam* is not referring to the physical universe. It is referring to the study of Torah. Therefore, "If one starts contemplating nature before having studied Torah, such meditation is not conducive at all to *ahavas ha'borei*." Ahron Soloveichik, *Logic of the Heart, Logic of the Mind: Wisdom and Reflections on topics of our times* (Genesis Jerusalem Press, 1991), p. 39.

KEEPING GOD IN MIND

Observing and appreciating nature may not automatically bring one closer to God. There must be an a priori recognition of God as the Source and continual Master of the world. With this recognition, the world around us is enhanced.

This can be explained with the following metaphor: If you were to take a zero and place a zero before it, it's still zero. Yet, if you add a one in front of the zeros, each added zero increases the value of the number.[9] From a spiritual perspective, the physical may be perceived as zero, but if we put God (the One) in front, the zeros now have tremendous value. This is why we recite blessings upon seeing and enjoying the physical world. Thinking of God transforms the experience so that the experience itself enhances the connection to God.

Associating the world with God makes the world itself a constant reminder of God. The mitzvah of tzitzis is a beautiful example of this. Regarding looking at one's tzitzis, the Talmud states:

> *Seeing leads to remembering. Remembering leads to action...Rabbi Meir said, "Why was techeiles (blue) chosen [to be the color for the tzitzis]? Because it resembles the sea, the sea resembles the sky, and the sky connects us to the One above.*[10]

One may ask: Why does Rabbi Meir mention water? If the water is the same color as the sky, we can make the connection from the blue of the *techeiles* to the sky itself and from the sky to the throne of God. Water appears like an unnecessary extra step in the process.

---

9   Heard from Rabbi Avraham Rivlin.
10   *Menachos* 43b.

Perhaps Rabbi Meir includes water to create as many positive associations as possible.[11] Not only will the strings of the tzitzis remind us of God, but every time we drink water or look at water, we can be reminded of God as well. Everything in the world is an extension of God. Moreover, since the Torah is the blueprint of the world,[12] properly connecting to the world also connects us to God's Torah.[13]

A BROAD LIFE

When we are not directly involved in mitzvos, it can be easier to forget about God. But God is not only found in the seemingly spiritual places and moments. He is everywhere. "Rabbi Yehoshua ben Levi said: If a person asks, 'Where is your God?' tell him, 'In the great metropolis of Rome.'"[14]

Sometimes, when we are in the "Rome" parts of life, we forget God. But there is no need to compartmentalize life as containing spiritual modes and mundane modes. Every moment of life has the potential for spirituality.

In response to a student who was struggling with finding meaning in his "secular" career, Rabbi Yitzchok Hutner metaphorically explained that someone who rents a room in a house as a primary residence and a room in a hotel to live as a guest is leading a double life. In contrast, renting a home with two rooms is symbolic of a "broad life, not double life." Despite the tendency to compartmentalize

---

11 *Rashi* there explains that mentioning the sea will remind one of the miracles that God performed by the sea. *Rashi* in *Sotah* 17a states that the sea is mentioned first because its color is more similar to *techeiles* than the sky is. See also *Kli Yakar*, *Bamidbar* 15:38.

12 See *Nefesh Hachaim*, chap. 4. In the Chazon Ish's *Faith and Trust (Emunah U'Bitachon)*, "Mussar and Halachah," chap. 30, he explains that it is not that man is influenced by bribes and therefore the Torah forbids it. Rather, since God looked into the Torah and created the world, the prohibition itself creates the reality of bribes having an influence on people's judgment.

13 One can argue that connecting to the Torah is clearly a more direct connection. Though this is true, there are many situations in life when one cannot connect in this manner.

14 *Yerushalmi*, *Taanis* 1:1. Heard from Rabbi Moshe Weinberger.

different aspects of life, we should strive to live a holistic life of *avodas Hashem*.[15] The more mindful we are of the spirituality in the now, the easier it will be to live such a life.

The *Rema* begins his commentary on the *Shulchan Aruch*: "'I have placed (*shivisi*) God before me constantly' (*Tehillim* 16:8)—this is a most important principle of the Torah and the attribute of the righteous ones." The Baal Shem Tov explained:[16]

> *Shivisi is related to hishtavus (equanimity). Whatever happens to a person should be treated the same—whether others praise or disgrace him. This applies to all things. When it comes to eating, it should make no difference whether one eats tasty food or not...One should recognize that everything that occurs to him is from God...God wants us to serve Him in every circumstance. When a person is speaking to others and cannot learn, he should be thinking of God. Similarly, there are times when a person will be on the road and will be unable to pray and learn like usual. In times like these, he can serve God in a different way. One should not be pained by this, because God wants us to serve Him in many different ways. Sometimes in this way and sometimes in that.*[17]

---

15   *Pachad Yitzchak: Igros U'Michtavim*, Letter 94. (p. 184). In the latter part of the letter, Rabbi Hutner explains the statement of *Sumchos*, "Whoever extends the *echad* [of *Shema*] will have length of days" (*Berachos* 13b), as referring to living a unified life of serving God. "Length of days" need not only be referring to living longer. It can also be referring to adding meaningful moments to life, which occurs when we live a more unified life.

16   *Keser Shem Tov* 220:1.

17   Part of this translation was adapted from David Sears, *Path of the Baal Shem Tov: Early Chasidic Teachings and Customs* (Jason Aronson, Inc., 1996).

Godliness can be found anywhere—and in all of our actions. We just need to open our eyes, ears, and heart. We need to be mindful.

PRIORITIZING SPIRITUALITY

Mindfulness of the world can enhance our relationship with God. Yet, such a perspective requires clarification. For example, going to a restaurant with one's wife can be understood in two different ways. One person chooses to go to the restaurant to enjoy the delicious food, and his wife is the most enjoyable companion with whom to share this experience. Another person wants to spend time with his wife to strengthen their relationship, and the restaurant is a mere catalyst for togetherness.

Similarly, life in this world can be viewed in a similar lens: Is religion a means to live this world more fully, or is this world a means for us to fulfill a greater purpose? A religious Jew's primary focus should be the spiritual self; the physical should be subsidiary to the spiritual.[18] As Rabbi Aharon Lichtenstein writes:

> *Yihud Hashem means simply that religion alone has absolute and comprehensive value. Everything else, no matter how socially or intellectually desirable, has only relative and secondary importance. Its worth is derived solely from the extent to which it contributes, however remotely, to the fulfillment of the Divine will. On this point there can be no compromise and should be no misunderstanding. A man's religion means everything or it means nothing."*[19]

---

18   Rabbeinu Bachya ibn Pakuda writes in *Chovos Halevavos*, chap. 3, "Gate of Self-Accounting," that one of the wise men said: "As water and fire cannot abide together in one vessel, so too, love for this world and love for the next cannot dwell together in the heart of the believer…this world and the next are like two rival wives: mollify one, you antagonize the other."

19   Lichtenstein, *Leaves of Faith*, p. 90. The last line from this quotation may be misunderstood as implying that religious practice is all-or-nothing. This is incorrect. Even

While recognizing the Divine in nature may enhance the experience, the primary goal is to enhance the relationship with God. God should not be an external force we choose to bring into our lives. Godliness should be part of everyday living. The physical world pulls us away from this recognition. Therefore, we need reminders. These reminders are built into our religion—but we need to be mindful of them. Experiences are not enough. We need to be reflective. Reflecting on experience can be more significant than the experience itself.

T R Y :

Note: As mentioned earlier, this book is a combination of ideals to aspire toward, as well as a guide that shows how to practically implement these ideals into daily living. While an ideal level may be to discern God in every facet of the physical, some may find it overwhelming to be constantly mindful of God (see chapter 11, "Can You Be Too Mindful?").

With some, the overwhelming feeling is due to their spiritual baggage of relating to God as overly harsh. If this is one's image, then constant awareness will be unpleasant and unsustainable. In contrast, viewing God as a loving and compassionate Father leads to experiencing the awareness of His presence as comforting and empowering.

The first three exercises address being more mindful of the world itself. These exercises also promote the value of enhancing emotional well-being. At your own pace, you can try to be more mindful of God in the physical world (these suggestions are found in parentheses).

---

when accepting upon oneself the religious path, it is understood that there will be ups and downs. There will inevitably be times when one does not act like their ideal self. Authentic growth usually progresses slowly. Rather, Rabbi Lichtenstein is saying that religion must be of primary importance and encompass all aspects of life. Otherwise, it's not much of a religion.

1. Try eating more mindfully. Try eating slowly and fully noticing what the food looks like, feels like, and tastes like. Try to pay attention to how it feels going through the body. Try to avoid eating during other activities. You will not only improve your health and self-regulation, but will also enjoy your food more. Rebbe Nachman of Breslov writes: "Whenever possible, avoid eating in a hurry. Even at home, don't gobble up your food. Eating is an act of holiness. It requires full presence of mind."[20] (Before eating, as you say the blessing, try to remind yourself Who allowed you to have this food. As you eat, remind yourself Who allowed you to enjoy this food.) [21]

> *There is a Yiddish story written solely about an orange. It is called "The Morantz" (The Orange), and it tells of an orange that was received as a present on Purim in Russia. Oranges in that part of the world were rare in the 1800s. The first day, people from all over town came to look at it. Wow! What an unbelievable sight! The second day, they came to smell it—an incredible aroma. The next day, they peeled it, saving each piece of peel with care in order to make marmalade. Then they divided the sections of the orange and crushed it in their mouths, feeling the delicious juices. An incredible experience. And then they had the marmalade that lasted for weeks. A memory for a lifetime—the orange.[22]*

---

20 Moshe Mykoff, *The Empty Chair: Finding Hope and Joy—Timeless Wisdom from a Hasidic Master, Rebbe Nachman of Breslov* (Jewish Lights, 1996), p. 25.

21 See Naomi Ross's article, "Foodie Nation: A Jewish Conversation on Mindful Eating," *Jewish Action*, Winter 2018.

22 Found in *Kol Yaakov* by Rabbi Boruch Leff, www.aish.com/tp/i/ky/48942556.html.

Even the eating of an orange can be an unbelievable experience—we just need to pay attention. Enhancing the experience can increase our love for God.

2. The next time you walk outside, pay attention to the beauty around you. If you see a tree, try to notice the variety of details of the tree: The way the light reflects on the tree; the way the tree moves with the wind; the sound of the wind itself. Notice the complexity and details of the world around you. (Remind yourself of the artist who created these beautiful masterpieces.)

3. Wherever you are right now, try to notice something small in front of you. It can be a tissue or a cup. Mindfulness does not need to be limited to what most refer to as beautiful. We can find beauty in objects that we may have initially failed to fully appreciate. Notice the details of the seemingly mundane object. Recognize the beauty in the mundane and even in what may be considered ugly. When we peer into "ugliness," we may be surprised to find that the deeper we look into it, the more we recognize its beauty.

4. Try reading the second chapter of the *Chovos Halevavos*, "*Shaar Habechinah*," or the beginning of *Emunah U'Bitachon* by the Chazon Ish. They contain beautiful descriptions of God's magnificent world and how it brings us closer to Him.

CHAPTER 13

Mindfulness and Mitzvos

E motions can hijack the brain.[1] Anger can lead to speaking irrationally. Desire can lead a person to sacrifice years of hard work for seconds of pleasure. Because emotions can distort our thinking, we need anchors. We need reminders of how we should be living. Mitzvos are the anchors that guide us back to what the soul truly wants. They connect us back to God.

In fact, in addition to meaning "commandment," the word "mitzvah" also means "connection."[2] Therefore, let us explore how specific mitzvos connect us to God.

MITZVOS AS REMINDERS

A social psychology experiment sought to explore ways to increase the likelihood of people leaving tips after a meal. One study found that tips were seventeen percent higher when the bill was placed on

---

1   This idea is based on the term, "amygdala hijack," coined by psychologist Daniel Goleman in *Emotional Intelligence: Why It Can Matter More Than IQ* (Bantam, 2005). The amygdala is the part of the brain mostly responsible for the emotional response.

2   *Shelah HaKadosh, Yoma, Derech Chaim.*

a heart-shaped plate instead of a circle-shaped plate.[3] Small reminders of love increase pro-social behavior. Remembering God's love for us increases the likelihood that we will behave properly.

This idea is illustrated in the *Rambam*'s description of the mitzvah of mezuzah. He writes:

> *A person must be vigilant in [the mitzvah of] mezuzah because it is an obligation which is constantly incumbent upon everyone. [Through its observance,] whenever a person enters or leaves [the house], he will encounter the unity of the name of the Holy One, blessed be He, and remember his love for Him. Thus, he will awake from his sleep and his involvement in vain matters, and recognize that there is nothing which lasts for eternity except the knowledge of the Creator of the world. This will motivate him to regain full awareness and follow the paths of the upright. The Sages said: Whoever wears tefillin on his head and arm, wears tzitzis on his garment, and has a mezuzah on his entrance, can be assured that he will not sin, because he has many reminders....*[4]

We need mitzvos to be mindful of God; the implication is that without such reminders, we are likely to forget. Because it is human nature to be pulled away from Godly living, we need to constantly draw ourselves back to the life of meaning.

---

3 Nicolas Guéguen, "Helping with all your heart: the effect of cardioid dishes on tipping behavior," *Journal of Applied Social Psychology* 43, no. 8 (2013): 1745–1749.

4 *Mishneh Torah, Hilchos Mezuzah*, 6:13. Translation adapted from Eliyahu Touger, *Mishneh Torah* (Moznaim Publishing Corporation, 1989).

REDIRECTING THE PHYSICAL

Mitzvos uplift the physical. The Talmud states:

> *Rabbi Meir used to say, a person is obligated to recite one hundred blessings daily, as it is written: "And now, Yisrael, what (mah) does Hashem, your God, ask of you? Only to fear him."*[5]

Rashi explains that Rabbi Meir reads the word *mah* (what) as *me'ah* (one hundred), thereby teaching that we should make one hundred blessings a day. This is not merely an alternative explanation of the verse. Rather, both ideas are to be read together. Rabbi Meir is teaching us that the path to fearing God is via saying one hundred blessings a day.[6] Before we eat, we say a blessing; when we hear thunder, we say a blessing; when we do a mitzvah, we say a blessing. Every aspect of life contains the potential to reconnect with God.[7]

SHABBOS—THE DAY OF BEING

Shabbos is a day to cease from doing and to just be. A day to be with yourself, your family, and God. Still, it is not a time for passivity; it is a time of positive growth.[8]

When the Torah describes the creation of the world, it states that God concluded the creation of the world on the seventh day. Creation did not end on the sixth day, because there was still something left to be created—*menuchah* (rest).[9] A simple translation of the word

---

5   *Menachos* 43b.

6   This idea is based on an essay from Rabbi Mayer Twersky found at http://torahweb.org/torah/2001/parsha/rtwe_bo.html.

7   Rabbi Tzadok HaKohen writes (*Tzidkas Hatzaddik* 2–3) that the purpose of *berachos* is to imbue the awareness of God into our different actions. He explains that this is also the essence of the mitzvah of *k'rias Shema*—to think about God in the morning and at night.

8   This idea is elaborated upon in Rabbi Friedlander's *Sifsei Chaim, Middoes V'Avodas Hashem*, vol. 2, p. 21.

9   See *Rashi* 2:2.

menuchah may be defined as a "lack of work"—but the lack of work should not require creating. Therefore, a more appropriate definition of *menuchah* is a "mindful rest."

The non-doing mode of mindfulness is more than doing nothing. In the non-doing of mindfulness, there is a conscious intention to attend to the present moment. Shabbos too is more than a day of doing nothing. It is not a day off; it is a day on. There needs to be an active intention to get closer to God on Shabbos. We need to be mindful to be mindful. True spirituality rarely arrives on its own—we must seek it.

Shabbos is a taste of *Olam Haba*.[10] Just like this world is a corridor for the next world, the week is the corridor for Shabbos. Our effort in this world prepares us for the next world, and the work of the week prepares us for Shabbos. As the Talmud states: "He who works before Shabbos will eat on Shabbos."[11] However, Shabbos is not just a goal; it is also a means. The being mode of Shabbos gives strength for the week. We need to do in order to be and we need to be in order to do. Shabbos provides us the opportunity to temporarily move aside from the journey in order to observe it. By obtaining a taste of the destination, we gain perspective for the journey. As Rabbi Dessler writes: "The real blessing of Shabbos is the expansion of one's consciousness from preoccupation with the trivialities of this world to immersion in the spiritual world."[12]

---

10   *Berachos* 57b (the Talmud states that Shabbos is one sixtieth of *Olam Haba*). This paragraph was inspired by a conversation with Dr. Yitzi Shechter. See *Michtav Me'Eliyahu*, vol. 2.

11   *Avodah Zarah* 3a. *Rashi* interprets this as saying that one who works in this world will benefit in the next world.

12   Dessler, *Strive for Truth* 4:6.

The being mode of Shabbos provides us the opportunity to reorient ourselves to what is truly important.

<hr />

Shabbos is a sign between us and God.[13]

A sign can have several purposes. For example, when a woman wears a wedding band, the very wearing of the band demonstrates to herself and to others that she is in a committed relationship. But it does more than that. It serves as a reminder of the relationship itself. Accordingly, keeping Shabbos demonstrates that we are people committed to God.[14] However, perhaps it is not just a sign claiming who we are, but it is a sign to remind us who we are. Shabbos is the sign that reminds us of God. Like any father who loves his child, He doesn't want us to forget about Him.

MITZVOS REQUIRE MINDFULNESS

> *The Lord said, "Inasmuch as this people has drawn close, with its mouth and with its lips it has honored Me, yet it has distanced its heart from Me—their fear of Me is like rote learning of human commands."[15]*

Not only can we forget God when it comes to physical matters, we can even forget God when it comes to spiritual matters. We can be observing without observing.

> *A baal teshuvah asked a certain rav, "It seems like I'm the only one who's excited when putting on tefillin. Why is this?" The rav responded, "You grew up in an environment not knowing any better, and now you are fortunate to see*

---

13   *Shemos* 31:13.
14   See *Chafetz Chaim Al HaTorah, Shemos* 31:13.
15   *Yeshayahu* 29:13.

the beauty of Judaism and practice accordingly. But many religious Jews also grew up in an environment of not knowing any better—they were taught to observe mitzvos by rote. In some ways, that is even harder to change."

It may be harder to change, but it can still change. Just like eating mindfully changes the experience, so too, performing mitzvos mindfully uplifts the experience. Mitzvos are a pathway to mindfulness, but they also require mindfulness.

Rabbi Shimon Schwab recalled the following from the Shabbos he spent with the Chafetz Chaim.

On Friday night, the Chafetz Chaim asked, "We know that the taste of the mann (food in the desert) was dependent on a person's thoughts, but what happened if you weren't thinking about anything?" After a few moments of silence, the Chafetz Chaim answered, "If you don't think, there is no taste."[16]

The holiness of a matter is related to how we attend to it. If we want to taste the beauty in mitzvos, we have to be mindful of the action itself and of the meaning in the action.

T R Y :

1. Try to use the small blessings throughout the day as a way to remind yourself of God. It is a common phenomenon for people to rush through the blessings on foods and the blessing for after going to the bathroom. However, spending a few

---

16   *Maayan Bais Hasho'eivah* (Mesorah Publication, 1994), p. 175.

extra seconds reciting them mindfully can be a wonderful opportunity to reorient ourselves toward our values.

2. Try to use the mezuzah or tzitzis as opportunities to remind yourself of God and how you want to live. Remember, awareness does not happen on its own.

3. Try to follow the advice of Rebbe Elimelech of Lizhensk:

> Whenever you perform any deed, whether Torah study, prayer, or positive commandments, you should familiarize yourself with the following words and make it a habit to recite them: I am hereby doing this in order to unify the Holy One Blessed Be He and the Divine Presence, to give delight to the blessed Creator.[17]

---

17 *Tzettel Katan* 4.

CHAPTER 14

Mindfulness and Prayer

The early pious ones would wait one hour
and then pray in order to direct
their hearts to God.

Berachos 32b

It can be difficult to immediately catapult oneself into a state of mindfulness. Mindfulness is a process. It is recommended to first sit down, pay attention to one's breath, and slowly move outward. Similarly, it can be difficult to jump into prayer. Perhaps it is for this reason that the pious ones set aside an hour before prayer. They set aside a fixed time to slow down and pay attention.

Engaging in a formal mindfulness practice prepares us to be more present in whatever we are doing. When therapists completed a five-minute mindfulness exercise before sessions, they reported being more present, and clients reported finding the sessions more effective.[1] Correspondingly, preparing before prayer assists in being more present with God. This idea is alluded to in the *Mesilas Yesharim* where the *Ramchal* discusses how to acquire purity:

> *One of the means that leads a person to acquire this trait is to prepare oneself for Divine service and mitzvos. This means that one should not suddenly enter into performing a mitzvah. Because [when he does so], his mind is not yet composed and he is unable to think about what he is doing. Rather, he should prepare himself and slowly prepare his heart for reflection.*

Preparing ourselves properly assists in being more attentive when we pray. Upon being present, we can be more aware of the words we are saying and to Whom we are saying them.

THE PRAYER EXPERIENCE

Mindfulness not only helps with preparing for prayer, but it helps with prayer itself. It is very possible to be engaged in a behavior without paying attention to it. For example, I can drink a cup of water and not even notice its taste or the way it feels traveling through the body. Accordingly, it is possible to pray without even experiencing the words we are saying. Therefore, the first step to praying properly is to attend to the present moment; to be mindful of our physical sensations, thoughts, and surroundings.

Upon being mindful, we can now choose how we want to direct attention. This is what we usually refer to as *kavanah*.[2] To gain a

---

1   Rose Dunn, Jennifer L. Callahan, Joshua K. Swift, and Mariana Ivanovic, "Effects of pre-session centering for therapists on session presence and effectiveness," *Psychotherapy Research* 23, no. 1 (2013): 78–85.

2   See *Mishnah Berurah* 60:7. He explains that there are two primary *kavanos* with mitzvos: (1) *kavanah* to be aware that one is doing a mitzvah, e.g., saying a blessing because this is the will of God; and (2) *kavanah* within the mitzvah itself, e.g., understanding the words

greater appreciation of the role and method of *kavanah* during prayer, let us read the following *Rambam*. He writes:

> *Kavanah: What is implied?*
>
> *Any prayer that is not [recited] with kavanah is not prayer.*[3]
> *If one prays without kavanah, he must repeat his prayers with kavanah. One who is in a confused or troubled state may not pray until he composes himself.*
>
> *What is meant by kavanah?*
>
> *One should clear his mind from all thoughts and envision himself as standing before the Divine Presence. Therefore, one must wait a short while before praying in order to focus his attention and then pray in a calm and supplicatory fashion. One should not pray as one carrying a burden who throws it off and walks away. Therefore, one must sit a short while after praying, and then withdraw. The pious ones of the previous generations would wait an hour before praying and an hour after praying. They would [also] extend their prayers for an hour.*[4]

---

of the blessing. With specific mitzvos, there is also the *kavanah* to fulfill that specific mitzvah, i.e., it is not enough to merely know that I am doing the will of God; rather, I am intending to fulfill this specific mitzvah.

3   According to Rabbi Joseph Soloveitchik, even the opinions that mitzvos do not need *kavanah* would agree that "*kavanah*, related to prayer, is, unlike the *kavanah* concerning other mitzvah performances, not an extraneous addendum but the very core of prayer" (Joseph B. Soloveitchik, "The Lonely Man of Faith," *Tradition: A Journal of Orthodox Jewish Thought* 7:2, [1965], 35). Rabbi Soloveitchik's grandfather, Rabbi Hayyim, expounds on the different aspects of *kavanah* in prayer in his commentary on the *Rambam* (*Chiddushei Rabbeinu Chaim HaLevi, Hilchos Tefillah* 4:1).

4   *Mishneh Torah, Hilchos Tefillah* (4:15–16).

According to the *Rambam, kavanah* requires preparation. It requires an initial effort to compose oneself and to think about God.[5] In prayer, we strive to attend to the present moment and to God.

The Jewish value of mindfulness is more than just being present to experience. It includes intentionally directing attention toward God. Therefore, *kavanah* can be understood as more than noticing experience; it includes being a participant. For example, when we drink a cup of water and notice the way the water tastes and how it feels flowing through the body, we are being mindful. *Kavanah* takes this a step further. With *kavanah*, we are not just noticing the experience, but we are thinking of how it helps us live better. We can also think of the One who enables us to enjoy the water. Intentional thinking transforms the experience itself.

TRANSCENDENCE IN PRAYER

As intention in prayer increases, so does the possibility of transcendence. As inferred from the *Shulchan Aruch*'s laws on prayer, this is something we should strive for. He states:

> *The pious ones and the men of deeds would seclude themselves (misbodedim) and concentrate on their prayers until they achieved the falling away of their physicality and the enhancement of their consciousness…*[6]

---

5   The fact that *kavanah* requires much preparation signifies how challenging it is. An interesting illustration of this challenge is described in the *Yerushalmi* in *Berachos* (Vilna ed., 2:4): "Rabbi Chiya said, 'I have never concentrated on prayer all of my days. Once I tried to concentrate, but all I could think about was politics.' Shmuel said, 'During prayer, I count the clouds.' Rabbi Bun Bar Chiya said, 'I count the stones in the wall when I should be praying.' Rabbi Matnaya said, 'I am grateful to my head, because it knows to bow automatically when we reach the *Modim* prayer.'" See *Pri Tzaddik, Parashas Vayeishev* 3, for a beautiful interpretation of the *Yerushalmi*.

6   *Orach Chaim* 98:1.

The pious ones were so focused on their prayers and aware of their consciousness that they temporarily distanced themselves from the physical. This was achieved through *hisbodedus*, seclusion.

What does it mean to use seclusion as preparation for prayer?

Rabbi Avraham ben HaRambam describes two forms of seclusion: *external* and *internal*.[7] External isolation is physically separating oneself. Internal isolation consists of quieting the physical and re-orienting one's entire self toward God. Internal isolation prepares us for prayer.

Mindfulness helps develop internal isolation. It helps us transcend. When we notice our experience, we are able to separate our consciousness from the active mind and from the physical. For example, as you are reading this, notice your body and notice your mind. When we notice our experience, and we are aware that we are noticing, we are able to create a distance between the consciousness and the physical. We can be an observer of physical experiences as opposed to being in them. The falling away of the physical occurs with the enhancement of the consciousness.

STAYING GROUNDED

It is important to note one should be careful when using mindfulness meditation exercises as a form of transcendence—there may be side effects.[8] Transcendence can lead to feelings of dissociation, depersonalization, and anxiety related to feeling detached from the body and reality. Observing experience in a healthy way is viewing it from a specific point; one is at home with the self, one is grounded. In unhealthy dissociation, there is no "I"; there is no grounded self. The person is dissociating from nowhere. It is the difference between

---

7   *Sefer Hamaspik L'Ovdei Hashem*, "*Hisbodedus*."

8   Alberto Perez-De-Albeniz and Jeremy Holmes, "Meditation: concepts, effects and uses in therapy," *International Journal of Psychotherapy* 5.1 (2000): 49–58.

observing waves from the safety of the shore versus observing them while swirling in the ocean. The latter experience can be unsettling and scary.

When observing experience in a healthy way, we are still able to connect to the experience. It is like holding the string of a kite versus seeing a kite fly away. Dissociation is when the experience is not grounded—the kite is flying away—and there is a disconnect between the person and the experience. In a healthy mindful state, we can hold the string of the kite. We can feel the kite without it overtaking us. We can be mindful of anxious thoughts and physical sensations and still feel them. Being mindful can even intensify the experience. When we are mindful of sad thoughts, we are more likely to cry.

PRAYING WITH YOUR FEET ON THE GROUND

In prayer, we can transcend ourselves without losing ourselves. This dialectic is beautifully illustrated in Rabbi Shimon's Schwab's *Iyun Tefillah*. He states:

> *When one stands before Hakadosh Baruch Hu (Holy One Blessed Be He) in tefilla and places his feet together as one, emulating the melachim, he is expressing the thought that he is relinquishing his free will and thus offering himself as a korban (sacrifice) to Hakadosh Baruch Hu. In so doing, he has performed the greatest act of free choice of which a human being is capable: that of voluntarily relinquishing that choice to Hakadosh Baruch Hu...Notwithstanding the fact that we relinquish our free will to Hakadosh Baruch Hu and are offering ourselves as a korban to Him, Hakadosh Baruch Hu does not want us to leave this world. On the contrary, Hakadosh Baruch Hu wants us to be alive in this world; He wants us to live our lives in accordance with His will. This thought is expressed in Maariv; He keeps us alive*

and does not allow our feet to slip. By living our lives here in
this world in accordance with His will, and by dedicating our
lives to Him and longing for Him, our lives have, in effect
become a living korban to Hakadosh Baruch Hu.[9]

With prayer, we are offering ourselves to God. But giving ourselves
to God is not through leaving this world. It is through being fully
present in this world. It is through "living our lives *here* in this world
in accordance with His will." The challenge of prayer is to have our
feet on the ground and reach the heavens.[10]

GROWTH THROUGH PRAYER

Being mindful in prayer is difficult. The nature of the mind is to
quickly wander. However, finding significance in the present moment decreases the likelihood of wandering. Therefore, gaining a
deeper appreciation of prayer can hopefully increase our ability to be
present when praying.

What is prayer?[11.]

- Is prayer focused on praising God?
- Is it a time for self-reflection?

---

9   Rabbi Shimon Schwab, *Rav Schwab on Prayer* (Brooklyn, NY: Mesorah Publications, 2001), p. 411.

10   See chapter 7, "Mindful Relationships," where we discussed that you can only truly care for another when you first have a sense of self. In *The Lonely Man of Faith*, Rabbi Soloveitchik describes the dialectic of finding oneself and giving up oneself in prayer. He writes (p. 75, note 2):

It should nevertheless be pointed out that the awareness required by the Halakhah during the recital of the first verse of *Shema* and that which accompanies the act of praying (the recital of the first benediction) are related to two different ideas. During the recital of *Shema* man ideally feels totally committed to God and his awareness is related to a normative end, assigning to man ontological legitimacy...On the other hand, the awareness which comes with prayer is rooted in man's experiencing his creatureliness and the absurdity embedded in his own existence...

11   Many of the ideas from this next section are adapted from Rabbi Yosef Zvi Rimon's *sefer*, *Tefillah: Pirkei Limud L'Naar.*

- Is it a time to request our needs?
- Is it each of these?

PRAYER AS SELF-REFLECTION

Rabbi Samson Raphael Hirsch writes that prayer is a time to examine and evaluate ourselves.[12] It is a time to be mindful of whether we are living according to our values. As we proceed through the various requests in the standard prayer, we are reminded of what we should be aspiring toward. In prayer, we ask for wisdom, forgiveness, and to become closer to God. We are reminded of what our *neshamah* truly wants. Prayer leads to reflecting on the gap between where we are and where we want to be. It is not only a time to look outward to God, but it is also a time to look inward. As Rabbi Menachem Mendel of Kotzk said, "People are accustomed to look at the heavens and to wonder what happens there. It would be better if they would look within themselves—to see what happens there."[13]

PRAYER AS CONNECTION

A person can spend an entire day with their spouse or child and not connect. Connection is not about physical proximity; it is about two individuals pausing and paying full attention to one another. One of the terms used for prayer is *pegiah*, a meeting. In *Bereishis Rabbah*, it states: "Why did God make the Matriarchs barren? Because He wanted their prayers." God loves us. Therefore, He wants us to slow down and designate a time to turn toward Him. Prayer is a time to be mindful and connect with *Avinu Malkeinu*, our Father, our King. Prayer is not just a means to better living—it is life itself.

---

12 Found in *Chorev*, beginning of *Pirkei Avodah*. He writes that this is manifest in the word used for prayer, *hispallel*. It is a reflexive language.

13 Simcha Raz, *The Sayings of Menahem Mendel of Kotsk* (Northvale, NJ: Jason Aronson, Inc., 1995), p. 2.

PRAYER AS REQUEST

"A person should first praise God and then pray" (*Berachos* 32b). Praise is a prelude to prayer. Before we ask God to help with our needs, we need to remind ourselves who God is and that He is in control.

Many will only turn to God when they are desperate. They will only turn to Him when someone is sick or when they are experiencing emotional or financial difficulties. We don't need to wait until the point of desperation. Reminding ourselves of God's omnipotence should lead to the recognition that we are always vulnerable; we are always desperate. God can instantaneously bring tragedy or liberation. Times of prosperity should not be taken for granted. We should pray for the blessings to continue.

Recognizing God's omnipotence will also lead to asking for help in the apparently minute aspects of life. If it's something we would ask a friend for help with, we can ask God too. For example, if we'll ask a friend for advice on where to buy a new suit, we can also ask God for help in finding the best suit for the best price. It would be foolish not to elicit the help of the One who is truly in control. No request is too small for God.

PRAYER AS PROCESS

Imparting the importance of prayer should lead to an increased effort in being present and focused on prayer. Still, it's a double-edged sword. The greater the importance placed on any behavior, the greater the guilt when not done well. In some cases, the anxiety of not doing it properly will negatively affect the behavior itself. Regarding prayer, there is a similar concern. While some apprehension is necessary in prayer, too much is detrimental. Too much anxiety about prayer will prevent one from really focusing on it.[14]

---

14   This is demonstrated in the Yerkes-Dodson Law which was discussed in chapter 11, "Can You Be Too Mindful?"

A metaphor by the *Kaf Hachaim* can help manage this anxiety. He writes: "If one is collecting pearls and accidentally loses one, he is not going to drop all the pearls to find the one he lost."[15] Similarly, when the mind is distracted during prayer, there is no benefit in being overly harsh on yourself. This will disturb the rest of prayer. Rather, you should try to focus on the words in front of you at the moment. You should continue to collect the pearls. In this vein, Rabbi Moshe of Kobryn related:

> *My teacher, Rabbi Mordecai of Lekhovitz, taught me how to pray. He instructed me as follows: "He who utters the word Lord [Elokeinu], and in doing so prepares to say King of the Universe [Melech Ha-Olam], is not speaking as he should. At the moment he says Elokeinu, he must think only of offering himself to the Lord, so that even if his soul should leave him at that moment, and he was not able to say Melech Ha-Olam it would be enough for him that he had been able to say Elokeinu."*[16]

It is the nature of the mind to wander. Berating ourselves for this may lead us to being engaged with guilt instead of being engaged with the words of prayer. The more adaptive response is to recognize that the mind wandered and to gently bring it back to the words we are saying. At times, the mind may go so far adrift that we can reach the end of *Shemoneh Esreh* without realizing where we've been. By cultivating mindfulness, we can improve our prayer experience. We

---

15   *Kaf Hachaim* 98:15. The Chafetz Chaim mentions a similar idea in the introduction to *Shemiras HaLashon*. He writes that if the *yetzer hara* tries to antagonize you for not saying *Retzei* properly, you should start afresh with *Modim*.

16   Buber, *Tales of Hasidim*, p. 153.

can catch ourselves earlier and more often when our minds drift. For example, during *Magen Avraham*, we may notice the mind has wandered and gently bring it back. Then, as we begin *Atah Chonen*, we may again notice the mind has drifted and gently bring it back, and so on. Although we would ideally prefer the mind not to wander at all, in the short term, we can at least learn how to recognize sooner when the mind is adrift. Being more aware of the wandering mind will lead to an overall net gain in paying attention.

Before we pray, let us pause. Let us pay attention to the breath, body, sounds, and thoughts. Upon centering ourselves, we can be more present to what we are saying and to Whom we are speaking. Rabbi Kook writes that the "difference between one who prays and one who doesn't is not just that one sanctified their time and the other did not—their entire day is different."[17] If we pray properly, the day is different. And if today is different, life is different.

T R Y :

1. Spend a few moments before prayer being mindful of your-self. Notice your breath, notice your body, notice the sounds, notice sight. Notice the feeling of the siddur in your hand. Notice the words inside the siddur. Spend a few moments being aware of where your mind is and how distracted you may be. As you notice the different thoughts, see if you can gently be aware of how you want to be spending the next few moments. Try to remind yourself of why you want to pray and how you want to pray.

2. As you pray, try to notice when the mind is wandering. When it wanders, there is no benefit to being too hard on yourself. Try to start afresh from that moment on. As the *Kaf Hachaim*

---

17   Introduction to *Olat Reiyah*, found in Rimon, *Tefillah: Pirkei Limud L'Naar.*

mentions, even if you missed some pearls, there are still so many more to pick up.

3. Use the word "*Atah*—You" as an anchor to bring the wandering mind back. Each time you say the word *Atah*, try to remind yourself to Whom you are speaking.

4. If you are praying with a minyan, clarify how you want to use those moments when most individuals let their minds drift (e.g., *chazaras ha'shatz*, *k'rias haTorah*). These are excellent times to work on your ability to sustain and increase attention. See if you can pay attention to the chazan's prayer and the significance of the prayer.

5. Remember the different aspects of prayer. It is a time for beseeching, a time for self-reflection, and a time for connection.

SPEAKING TO GOD THROUGH INFORMAL PRAYER

In addition to formal prayer, Judaism has a tradition of spontaneous prayer. God is always available to listen. Rebbe Nachman of Breslov would encourage people to set aside time to speak to God in their own language like they would to a close friend. He recommended that one should set aside at least an hour to speak to God and share whatever is on one's mind. There may even be times when one doesn't know what to say—and one can verbalize that too.[18] Breslover Chassidim often go into the forest to do this. Some will be walking and talking to God, while others will be sitting still with their eyes closed in silence. Such a practice can transform one's day.

There is no "right" way to be *misboded*. The key is to begin and to see where it takes you. It is a pathway to being more mindful of God. It is also a pathway to self-awareness. As we speak openly to God, we become more aware of what is frustrating us and what we are struggling with. Understanding what our challenges are is crucial

---

18   *Likutei Moharan Tinyana* 25.

to dealing with them. We cannot solve what we are not aware of. We cannot accept what we are not aware of.

During my orientation for graduate school, I was seated next to a well-known expert on schizophrenia. Before I drank a cup of water, I said a short blessing. When the professor gave me a funny look, I said, "Don't worry, I'm not talking to myself." "Then who were you talking to?" he asked. "I was talking to God," I responded. The professor was not impressed.

Unfortunately, many find talking to God awkward. This may be a reflection of God not being an integral part of their reality. The more we talk to God, the more He will be part of our reality. The more God is part of our reality, the easier it will be to talk to Him.

TRY

1. Set aside a few minutes a day in a secluded area to speak to God. Say whatever is on your mind. Rebbe Nachman of Breslov writes: "Even if you are completely removed from God, you should express your thoughts to Him, asking that He bring you back..."

2. If you are interested in exploring this further, try reading *Hishtapchus Hanefesh*, a compilation of the teachings of Rebbe Nachman of Breslov on *hisbodedus* (seclusion) and *hisbonenus* (contemplation). Part of this was translated into English by Rabbi Aryeh Kaplan, entitled *Outpouring of the Soul*.

3. Some may be interested in more intense meditation exercises. You may want to try Rabbi Aryeh Kaplan's *Jewish Meditation* or Rabbi DovBer Pinson's *Meditation and Judaism*. The Baal Shem Tov's recommendation was to do so with a

guide or colleague. This will help you feel grounded.[19] A guide or friend can help keep you grounded.

> *There is a story of two Chassidic masters, Rabbi Avraham and Rabbi Schneur Zalman of Liadi, that were engaged in a deep mystical study. All of a sudden, Reb Zalman noticed that Reb Avraham was slowly drifting away. He realized that his companion was being swallowed in the ecstasy of his experience. Hurriedly, Reb Zalman rushed to the kitchen to retrieve a bagel with butter. Upon returning, he handed Reb Avraham the bagel and forced him to have a bite. Subsequently, Reb Avraham returned to the mundane materialistic domain. The consumption of a physical object, the bagel, forced a rejoining of soul and body.[20]*

---

19   *Tzavoas HaRivash* 63.

20   DovBer Pinson, *Meditation and Judaism: Exploring the Jewish Meditative Paths* (Jason Aronson, Inc., 2004), p. 69.

CHAPTER 15

Mindfulness and Talmud Torah

> The one who does much and the one who does a little [are equal]—as long as his heart is directed toward Heaven.
>
> *Menachos* 13:11

Astudy at the University of California demonstrated that a two-week mindfulness training course significantly decreased mind-wandering and improved cognitive function and working memory.[1] Mindfulness improves concentration. The more we are present and notice when the mind is wandering, the sooner we can bring it back. The sooner we bring it back, the more we will attain and retain. Yet, mindfulness is much

---

1   Michael D. Mrazek, Michael S. Franklin, Dawa Tarchin Phillips, Benjamin Baird, and Jonathan W. Schooler, "Mindfulness training improves working memory capacity and GRE performance while reducing mind wandering," *Psychological Science* 24, no. 5 (2013): 776–781.

more than a concentration tool. Mindfulness reframes whatever we are doing. Let us explore how mindfulness enhances and deepens *talmud Torah.*

LEARNING IN THE PRESENT MOMENT

And these words, which I command you today, shall be upon your heart.[2]

The Chafetz Chaim comments on the above verse:

- "And these words"—When it comes to learning, you only need to focus on the page in front of you.
- "Which I command you"—In this moment, you should imagine that there is only you and God. Every person has the ability to uplift the world.
- "Today"—Focus on what you are doing now. This moment will never come again. In this moment, you have the ability to serve God to your utmost.
- "Shall be upon your heart"—These three ideas should constantly be on your heart.[3]

For many, the moment they begin learning, intrusions barge in. Some are reminded of all the different things they need to take care of; others experience a sense of sadness for having learned so little; and for some, learning leads to an overly intense pressure to accomplish as much as possible in the allotted time. The Chafetz Chaim advises us to focus on what's right in front of us in this very moment.

⊢————————⊣

2   *Devarim* 6:6.
3   *Chafetz Chaim Al HaTorah* 238.

The Talmud states: "A person should dedicate himself to Torah like an ox carries its yolk and a donkey its burden."[4]

Rabbi Yitzchak Joseph explains that when an ox plows, it does not care if the land will produce fruit. Its primary objective is to follow its master's wishes; it is focused on the plowing itself, not the results.[5] Similarly, in learning Torah, the primary objective should be to fulfill the will of God in that moment. It is not necessarily within our power to determine the fruits of our labor. Our job is to try our best with what is in front of us.

Many students struggle with being overly focused on the results of their learning. While there is value to this concern, it comes with side effects—it takes away from being present. They forget that there is much value in the process. The Talmud states: "[If someone says] I struggled but still did not discover, do not believe him."[6] Rabbi Menachem Mendel of Kotzk commented: "Since the struggle is itself valuable, it is indeed a great find."[7] Although obtaining knowledge is important, the primary emphasis in learning is the study itself.

The Vilna Gaon writes:

> *The wise man delights in his learning by the fact that he is fulfilling the will of his Creator...but the fool doesn't enjoy it until he finishes the book, and he rushes to finish it. Therefore, he will not find blessing in it.*[8]

---

4   *Avodah Zarah* 5b.
5   *Sefer Achas Sha'alti.* His comment was on the *Tanna D'bei Eliyahu* 22:5.
6   *Megillah* 6b.
7   *Amud Ha'emes* 150.
8   *Even Sheleimah* 8:4.

Modern society values tangible results. Effort itself doesn't make the news (unless it is associated with an accomplishment). Some may feel that to truly succeed in Torah one must become a prominent rabbi. Yet, according to the Vilna Gaon, *talmud Torah* is about using the given time to fulfill the will of God. As Rabbi Aharon Lichtenstein writes:

> *It is precisely for the effort, the process of the recherché (obscure), that the Halakhah presses most insistently. Of yedi'at Ha-Torah, the knowledge of Torah, Hazal has relatively little to say; but of talmud Torah, they can never say enough.*[9]

LEARNING WITH PATIENCE

Applying mindfulness to *talmud Torah* entails finding the value in the process. When we are more present and find more meaning in the now, we are less likely to feel pressured to rush to the next thing. We can study with patience—a vital component of *talmud Torah*.

It states in *Mishlei*: "Wisdom lies before an understanding person, but a fool's eyes are directed to the ends of the earth."[10] *Rashi* explains that the wise one is focused on that which is in front of him. The fool is overly focused on the future. The fool says, "How can I study *Seder Nezikin*, it is thirty chapters; *Keilim*, it's thirty chapters; *Shabbos*, twenty-four chapters?" The wise man says, "I will do two chapters today and two tomorrow." Growth in learning requires presence and patience.

The *Sefer Hachinuch* writes that Moshe spent forty days on Har Sinai to teach us that learning Torah takes time.[11] A while ago,

---

9   Rabbi Aharon Lichtenstein, *Leaves of Faith: The World of Jewish Learning* (KTAV Publishing House, 2003), vol.1, p. 90.
10   *Mishlei* 17:24.
11   *Sefer Hachinuch*, Introduction.

I had a study partner who learned slowly and methodically. It was not always easy studying with him. At times, I felt frustrated that we were not accomplishing much; yet, to this day, I remember more from what I studied with him than from what I studied with some of my other study partners. When we are less focused on success, we find success.

Rabbi Chaim Hakohen, a student of Rabbi Chaim Vital wrote:[12]

> *Chazal explain that one will be asked [after life in this world], "Did you establish set times for Torah study?" He will not be asked, "How much Torah did you study?" because better is the deliberate study of five chapters with pleasantness than ten [chapters] with pressure...*

DEPTH IN LEARNING

Learning slowly is not just about pace; it consists of studying with contemplation and self-awareness. It includes being honest with what we know and what we don't know. It requires humility. Successful learning requires one to ask, "Do I truly understand what the text is saying," "Do I truly understand what the other person is saying?"

Patience leads to depth. Depth is more than a deeper interpretation of a text. Depth is allowing the teaching to penetrate by being aware of what is occurring inside of us. At times, this can be more sacred than the learning itself. In Rabbi Kook's personal letters, he writes:

> *There are times that I cannot learn and I am pulled to boredom. This is because I need to turn to my inner thoughts or to my emotions which in that moment may be more sacred than the learning or other work.*[13]

---

12   *Mekor Chaim* 1:1:4. Initially seen in Rabbi Moshe Tzvi Weinberg, "Maintaining Peace of Mind in a High-Speed World," *Purim To Go*, 5773, Yeshiva University.

13   *Chadarav* 138.

This depth is independent of intellectual prowess. The mindful beginner's reflection may be deeper than the cerebral academic's insights.

TALMUD TORAH AS MINDFULNESS

Although the common definition of mindfulness relates to paying attention to the present moment, I believe that a Jewish definition of it is more expansive. Attending to the present moment is important, but it's not enough. A Jewish value of mindfulness includes paying attention to meaning in this moment, paying attention to God in this moment. Therefore, mindfulness doesn't just enhance *talmud Torah*, but *talmud Torah* is in itself a form of mindfulness. As Rabbi Pinchas Ben Yair writes: "Torah brings to watchfulness."[14] *Talmud Torah* can bring our consciousness closer to the truth, which is why it is associated with freedom: "There is nobody as free as one who is involved in Torah."[15] When we are engaged in Torah, when we are engaged in meaning in the moment, we are serene; we are not lacking anything—we are free.[16]

THE GREATER CONTEXT

Developing a mindful approach in learning includes the recognition that learning Torah is part of a greater life of *avodas Hashem*. Therefore, during the learning itself, it can be helpful to pause and reflect on the value of learning. Rabbi Chaim Volozhin states:

> Before learning Torah, a person should think about God with purity of heart and fear of Him, and cleanse himself with thoughts of repentance, so that He can connect and attach himself to the will of God when he learns. He should also

---

14　*Avodah Zarah* 20b.

15　*Avos* 6:2.

16　See *Nefesh Hachaim* 4:16–17.

accept upon himself to observe and fulfill all that is written in the entire Torah...he should pray that God will lead him to discover the truth of Torah...This should be done even in the middle of learning. Permission is given to interrupt regular learning subjects, for a short time, before the passion of the fear of God becomes extinguished from his heart, [to reignite] all that he accepted upon himself before he began learning. He should think again of the fear of God...This is not bitul Torah (wasting time), because it is necessary in order for the Torah to have a lasting impact.[17]

Viewing *talmud Torah* in the greater context of a life of *avodas Hashem* will not only enhance the learning, but it will also provide comfort when learning is difficult. When struggling in my own learning, I remind myself of my brother's Shavuos in the Intensive Care Unit.

Several years ago, my brother and his wife spent Shavuos in the hospital, taking care of their child. In addition to the health challenges their child was facing, there was the initial sadness of spending such a holy time in the hospital. Yet, upon further reflection, they were comforted by the recognition that this was where God wanted them to be. With an hour left of Yom Tov, my brother was on pace to finish a certain masechta, yet, at the moment, he decided that it was more important to spend the last hour of Yom Tov singing with his child. At that moment, he felt that God's desire was that he put down the Gemara.

Being a mindful Jew is recognizing that each moment of our lives contains a different mission. There was no reason why that Shavuos

---

17   Ibid., 4:7.

could not be on as high a level—if not higher—than any other Shavuos.[18]

Unfortunately, we sometimes think that if only certain circumstances would change, we could serve God so much better. This is not so. Serving God is doing what we can with what we're given. Truly living a life of *avodas Hashem* is about saying, "Ribbono Shel Olam (Master of the World), I'm not in control; You are. I will try to follow Your lead and do my best." Our job is to try our best in this moment, like an ox that serves its master.

TRY:

1. Try to be a little more mindful while you learn. While sitting with a *sefer* in front of you, notice your breath, notice the way your body is feeling. As you slowly open the *sefer*, notice the words on the page. Notice where your mind is. Perhaps you can say to yourself, "Ribbono Shel Olam, I want to spend the next number of minutes learning Your Torah to the best of my ability. Please let me learn as well as possible."

2. Try to follow the advice of the *Nefesh Hachaim* and pause every now and then in the middle of learning to reflect upon God and why you are learning.

3. Try to find a small insightful idea that you are going to learn very slowly. As you learn, pay extra attention to what is occurring within you.

4. As you conclude your learning, spend a few extra moments to reflect on what you just learned.

---

18 Understandably, it is still natural to be panged when missing religious opportunities. For example, although there were members of B'nei Yisrael that were exempted from the *korban Pesach* for legitimate reasons, they were still saddened by their inability to be involved in the mitzvah. Still, it is helpful to console oneself with the recognition that the current situation is part of a greater mission.

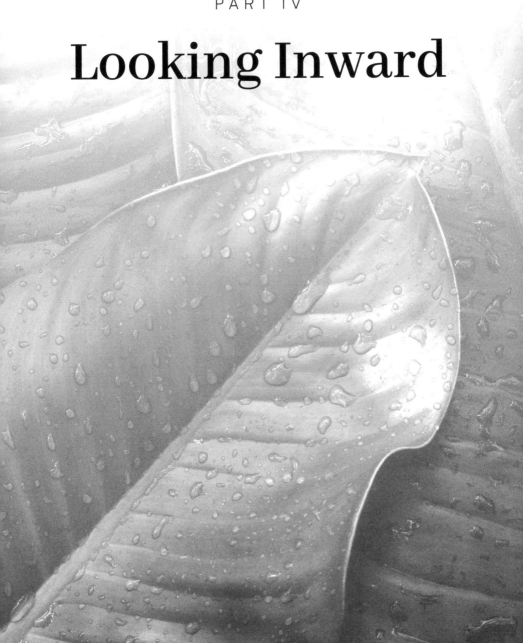

PART IV

Looking Inward

CHAPTER 16

Teshuvah

Even though the sounding of the shofar
on Rosh Hashanah is a decree, it contains
an allusion. It is as if it is saying,
"Sleepy ones, wake up from your
sleep...Evaluate your actions, repent,
and remember your Creator."[1]

Rambam

Waking up to the present moment forces us to face
reality. It forces us to face ourselves: our imperfections and mistakes. When facing a mistake, we have
a choice. The immediate, instinctual response is to
rationalize the behavior. This is easier; it saves us from admitting
defeat and the pain it brings. It saves us from taking a deeper look at
ourselves and dealing with the inner critic. However, the easier path
may not be the better one. Eating cake instead of exercising brings

---

1   *Mishneh Torah, Hilchos Teshuvah* 3:4.

pleasure in the moment, but it can later bring greater pain. When we pause and think, we are less driven by instinct and more likely to act according to our values. There is a scene in Antoine de Saint-Exupéry's *The Little Prince* that expresses this:

> *"Why are you drinking?" the little prince asked.*
>
> *"To forget," replied the drunkard.*
>
> *"To forget what?" inquired the little prince, who already was sorry for him.*
>
> *"Forget that I'm ashamed," confessed the drunkard, hanging his head.*
>
> *"What are you ashamed of?" inquired the little prince, who wanted to help.*
>
> *"Of drinking!" concluded the drunkard.*[2]

When we err, we can face the mistake or we can avoid it. A person who feels he has just wasted an hour on the computer may attempt to deal with his discomfort by going right back to the computer to distract himself. Refraining from returning to the computer requires sitting with discomfort.

Teshuvah (repentance) requires vulnerability. It requires facing weakness and admitting imperfection. The *Rambam* writes:

> *Among the paths of repentance is for the penitent to constantly call out before God, crying and entreating.*[3]

Where do these tears come from? What is the person crying for? It is the pain of looking at myself and saying, "I messed up," "I should have acted differently." We should not suppress the pain—it reveals

---

2   Antoine de Saint-Exupéry, *The Little Prince* (New York: Harcourt Inc., 1943), p. 35.

3   *Mishneh Torah, Hilchos Teshuvah* 2:4.

what we value. If it hurts, then it shows we care. *Teshuvah* done properly should be painful,[4] yet also beautiful. Saying sorry is difficult, yet rewarding.

Teshuvah means return. A return to ourselves—to be brutally honest with ourselves and what we value. A return to God—by admitting a mistake, we return to God's path. A simultaneous return to both—when we return to the self, we are returning to the Divine within, we are connecting with the Creator. In the words of Shlomo HaMelech, "The One who covers his sin will not succeed, but he that admits and leaves them will obtain mercy."[5]

LEARNING FROM MISTAKES

Facing our mistakes not only helps us return in the moment, it helps us learn from the mistake. Rabbeinu Bachya ibn Pakuda interprets the verse, "*Chacham einav b'rosho*,"[6] which is literally translated as "the wise man, his eyes are in his head," as saying that the wise man reflects on his beginning. He examines his past experiences.[7] We're all going to make mistakes. The difference between the fool

---

4   On the verse, "It is a Shabbos, a day of complete rest for you, and you should afflict yourselves; an eternal decree" (*Vayikra* 16:31), the *Abarbanel* comments that the *inui*, the pain of Yom Kippur, corresponds to the emotional pain of *teshuvah*. Heard from Rabbi Mayer Twersky, www.torahweb.org/torah/2015/parsha/rtwe_achrei.htm.

5   *Mishlei* 28:13. Rabbi Hirsch beautifully elaborates on this verse (*From the Wisdom of Mishlé*, p. 222):

Even the most depressing awareness—of having committed some wrong—does not irredeemably rob him of his good spirits. Once he has recognized his wrong deed, he tries not to cover it up and let it gnaw at him in the dark recesses of his subconscious. He knows such self-deception will get him nowhere. He rather views his act undisguisedly, in a clear light, admits it to himself and before God, and tries to make up for it as best as possible. Before God he earnestly promises to avoid such guilty acts in the future; and from this serious determination he regains the serenity that is essential to the fulfillment of our duty.

6   *Koheles* 2:14.

7   *Chovos Halevavos, Shaar Cheshbon Hanefesh* 3.

and the wise man is that the wise man makes new mistakes and the fool makes the same mistakes over and over again.

Delving too much into the past can be harmful, but the right amount can be motivating. There is a place for healthy guilt—it helps us learn from our mistakes. When Rabbeinu Bachya ibn Pakuda discusses pride, he explains that one of the ways we can tell the difference between healthy pride and unhealthy pride is by seeing what it leads to. Similarly, when it comes to guilt, if it motivates the person to improve, it's a healthy guilt. If it overwhelms and hinders the person's progress, then it's clearly not coming from a healthy place.

STARTING ANEW

Mindfulness enables us to be more aware of ourselves, to admit we have fallen, and to make space for the discomfort with that. But *teshuvah* does not end there. Mindfulness also helps us to rise anew and move beyond the mistake. Being mindful entails viewing the world with the beginner's mind, which we previously explained as the ability to begin each moment as if it's the first. Beginning again in this very moment prevents sins from hindering present and future service of God. "*And now*, Israel, what does Hashem, your God, ask of you but to fear Hashem, your God" (*Devarim* 10:12). The midrash states: "*Now* is a language of *teshuvah*."[8] The way to do repentance is to focus on the *now*.[9] *Teshuvah* entails focusing on what we can change and do in this very moment.

The midrash relates that when the Romans came to destroy the Beis Hamikdash, they asked one of the Jewish traitors, Yosef Mishisa, to guide them. Upon helping them, he was rewarded by being given permission to take whatever he wanted from the Beis

---

8   *Bereishis Rabbah* 21:6.

9   Perhaps the midrash can be interpreted in another manner. It doesn't just mean that being present assists *teshuvah*. Rather, being fully present to God and ourselves in this moment is in itself a part of *teshuvah*.

Hamikdash. When he chose the *Menorah*, the Romans said, "It is not appropriate for you to take this." They took it away and told him to take something else. But he refused. He said, "It was enough that I already angered God one time; should I anger Him again?"[10]

Yosef Mishisa did not let his past mistakes prevent him from eventually sacrificing his life for God. The past does not need to hold us back from serving God anew in this very moment, the most precious moment we have.

Distress about past misdeeds can make it difficult to move forward. Like the drunkard, we can be tempted to manage the pain of mistakes by distracting ourselves with more mistakes. Therefore, it is helpful to remember that once we have sincerely repented, we are considered new creations and can put our thoughts about past misdeeds behind.[11]

As Rabbeinu Yonah writes in his *Yesod Hateshuvah*:

> *On the day [the person repents] he should cast away all of his sins and consider himself as if he is born that day—having neither merit nor sin; and this day is the beginning of his deeds.*[12]

---

10 *Bereishis Rabbah* 27:27.

11 Interestingly, Rabbi Kook, in his *Orot Hateshuvah* (13:9), implies that even during the process of repentance, one should not overemphasize the past. He writes: "The foundation of repentance is to focus on fixing the future. In the beginning, one should not place too much of an emphasis on the past, for if he will try to repair it, he will find many obstacles and it will be difficult to become closer with God. However, if a person focuses on fixing his actions, he will also be given assistance from above in rectifying the past."

12 In Rabbeinu Yonah's statement, the perspective is from man. Man should view himself as if he is new. This isn't just providing a pragmatic perspective. This is the reality. The *Talmud Yerushalmi* states (*Rosh Hashanah* 21a): "God said to them: Since you went before Me in judgment on Rosh Hashanah and you left in peace, I consider you as if you are a new creation." Upon repenting, God considers us as if we were new.

Believing in God includes believing in the gift of *teshuvah*—the gift to start anew.

FINDING SATISFACTION IN THE PROCESS

Alcoholics Anonymous emphasizes living "one day at a time." For the alcoholic, the prospect of staying sober the rest of his life is overwhelming. Appreciating the value of staying sober today, independent of what will happen tomorrow, makes it more manageable. This concept can be applied to any area of self-improvement and especially *teshuvah*. Every small step toward God is valuable. It is not all or nothing.

> *After one Yom Kippur in the Mirrer Yeshiva, the students looked very down. The Mashgiach, Rabbi Chatzkel Levenstein, recognized that this was due to having had a beautiful Yom Kippur where they reached such high levels, and quickly afterward feeling like they were back to the same people they had been the day before Yom Kippur. He told them the following story: "There once was a king who was building a palace. He contracted the best designers, builders, and equipment, and after five years of working on the palace, it was coming to its closing stages. The king decided he wanted to put the finishing touch on the building, so he was going to install the final ornament that would rest on top of the palace. When the time arrived for the king to affix the ornament, the wind blew and knocked him down. The king started crying, "My palace has fallen, my palace has fallen." The people looked at the king with surprise and responded, "Just because you have fallen doesn't mean that what you built has also fallen."[13]*

---

13   Heard from Rabbi Matisyahu Salomon. At the end of the tape, he stated that even if one

Rav Chatzkel said that the Yom Kippur the students experienced and what they created with their powerful prayers will be part of the building waiting for them in the next world.[14] Just because they temporarily fell doesn't mean their efforts to refine themselves and to grow were in vain. On the contrary, every bit of effort we put into serving God has an eternal impact. The bricks we create in the now will always be ours.

RETURNING—AGAIN AND AGAIN

In mindfulness practices, we try to notice experience as opposed to simply going through it. It is the difference between watching the waves of one's thoughts, feelings, and sensations versus being in the waves. However, it is expected that there will be moments when we leave the place of observing. There are times when the waves will pull us away from the shore. When this happens, it is important not to be too hard on ourselves but rather to notice and compassionately bring ourselves back.[15] This may happen again and again. When we notice, we are already back. Every moment we are back is valuable in itself. In life, we try to stay on a certain path, but there are times when we veer from the proper path. We make mistakes. When that happens, we should notice that we wandered and gently bring ourselves back. Again, and again.

---

ends up committing a certain sin, he still gets rewarded for each moment he postponed it. Each moment is valuable, independent of what happens after.

14　Dr. Yitzi Schechter added that it is not just building bricks for the next world. Many of our positive behaviors are building bricks for this world as well. Each moment in life is enhanced by our previous positive moments.

15　From a behavioral perspective, this increases the likelihood of noticing the wandering. If you are hard on yourself, noticing is an aversive experience and is less likely to reoccur. Conversely, a compassionate response (and even a positive one) reinforces noticing.

T R Y :

1. Slow down and pay attention to yourself. Notice your breath, your body, and your mind. Let yourself think about any area in life you want to improve. Notice if there is any pain with that. When we think of what we want to improve, we are forced to confront the uncomfortable gap between where we are and where we want to be. Paying attention to the gap can bring up sadness and discomfort. To improve, we have to first be willing to stay with the discomfort. *Teshuvah* is about noticing and carrying the pain while still moving forward. In slowly stepping forward, we may be pained for not moving fast enough and not being further on the journey. In that moment, we must remind ourselves that the past need not hinder the present. We can only affect what is happening now. *Avodas Hashem* is about doing what we are supposed to be doing now. Each step forward, no matter how incremental, is no less great.

2. Try to encourage apologies. It is not uncommon to find someone apologizing to another and receiving the response, "You should be sorry. Do you realize what you did?" If that's the response, the person is less likely to apologize in the future. When someone else apologizes to you, try to receive it well and even thank them for the apology.

CHAPTER 17

Quiet

God was not in the wind...not in the
earthquake...not in the fire...[but]
in a still, small voice.

Melachim 19:11–12

I spent all my days among the wise,
and I have found nothing better
for a person than silence.

Avos 1:18

Two friends were walking outside and talking
until the conversation slowly died. In an effort
to break the silence, one said to the other, "Isn't
it uncomfortable that we're just walking without
talking to each other?" The friend responded, "I was just
enjoying looking at the trees."

Although they were both in the same situation, what was uncomfortable for one was a pleasant experience for the other. For many, sitting in silence is difficult—whether it be with oneself or another.

SITTING IN SILENCE

There is a value in sitting still and being in the moment. Yet, for many, setting aside time to *be* is aversive. Timothy Wilson, a social psychologist at the University of Virginia, along with his colleagues, recruited hundreds of college students and community volunteers to spend anywhere from six to fifteen minutes in a room alone. On average, participants did not enjoy the experience very much. In fact, in one of the studies, sixty-seven percent of the men chose to administer an electric shock to themselves during the fifteen-minute sitting period. They preferred painful stimulation over sitting in silence.[1]

Many have lost the ability to sit quietly and to give themselves time to think. Constant connection to devices doesn't help. Because the text message or email provides immediate stimulation to the brain, the brain becomes accustomed to this stimulation, thereby leading to discomfort when the stimulation is absent. This creates a dangerous negative cycle where people avoid the uncomfortable state of just being by seeking the next immediate stimulation or distraction. Ironically, they are only uncomfortable because they accustomed themselves to distractions.

Fortunately, we can learn how to adapt to this new reality. Just like smokers find that it is not so difficult to cease smoking on Shabbos, many report a similar phenomenon with cell phones. When the phone is not accessible, it is easier to refrain. A study at the University of Texas found that in a variety of cognitive tasks, participants who put

---

1   Timothy D. Wilson, David A. Reinhard, Erin C. Westgate, Daniel T. Gilbert, Nicole Ellerbeck, Cheryl Hahn, Casey L. Brown, and Adi Shaked, "Just think: The challenges of the disengaged mind," *Science* 345, no. 6192 (2014): 75–77.

their phones in a different room significantly outperformed participants who had their phones nearby. Researchers also found that the
more individuals are dependent on their cell phones, the more their
performance on cognitive tasks is affected. The "simple" solution
they recommend? Put the phone out of sight.[2]

IT'S OK TO BE QUIET

In 2012, Susan Cain published her bestseller, *Quiet: The Power of
Introverts in a World That Can't Stop Talking*. The book struck a chord
with many. The premise of the book is that society has over-idealized
the extrovert and pathologized the introvert. This has consequences.
People used to admire character; now they admire personality. In
many organizations, the ideas that are heard aren't necessarily the
best—they are the ones that come from the loudest or most charis-
matic voices.

The quiet voice can be overlooked; valuable ideas can be overlooked. Rabbeinu Nissim Gerondi explains that the reason God
afflicted Moshe with a speech impediment was so that people would
follow him for the content of his message and not for his eloquence.[3]

> *A patient described that when he applied for a position as a
> counselor in a camp, the director interviewing him said, "We
> need counselors who can be lively, stand up on the benches,
> and get the kids excited—does that fit you?" He answered,
> "By nature, I'm not very loud. If you need that, I'll push my-
> self, but there are usually already enough counselors doing
> that. If you want, I can be the counselor that helps the kid in
> the corner that no one notices."*

---

2   Adrian F. Ward, Kristen Duke, Ayelet Gneezy, and Maarten W. Bos, "Brain Drain: The
    Mere Presence of One's Own Smartphone Reduces Available Cognitive Capacity," *Journal
    of the Association for Consumer Research* 2, no. 2 (2017): 140–154.

3   *Derashos HaRan* 3.

He got the job. It's not only OK to be quiet; sometimes, that's exactly what's needed.[4]

SPEAK LESS, DO MORE

Shammai says in the Mishnah, "Say little and do much."[5] This statement can be understood in two ways. It can be read as encouraging two parallel recommendations—it is better to speak less and do more. Or, it can be read as a causative relationship: Speak less, and thereby, you will do more. Talking about important ideas can provide the illusion of accomplishment at the expense of real accomplishment. It is easier to talk of ideals than to live with ideals—but the latter is more important.

⊢————————————————⊣

With words, we can say whatever we'd like. Words have the potential for falsehood (even the words we say to ourselves). They distract us from experience; they can take us away from the truth. We can occasionally get so caught up in our descriptions that we lose touch with the way things are. For example, it is almost impossible to fully describe in words the experience of watching a sunset. The moment we put it into words, we are to some degree distorting the reality. In silence, we can be more mindful of the experience itself.

Even if words do not distort the truth, they can diminish an experience. One of the explanations for the effectiveness of psychotherapy is that speaking about experiences decreases the emotional intensity related to them. When it comes to unpleasant experiences, this can be necessary and helpful, but there are certain ideas that don't need

---

4   The lesson in the story isn't just that society should value quiet people. It is also teaching the importance of being honest with oneself in recognizing one's strengths and weaknesses.

5   *Avos* 1:15.

to be shared immediately. When something inspires us, sharing it immediately can take away from its ability to be internalized.

> *The Alter of Kelm once waited twenty-five years before sharing something with his students because he wanted to be sure that it had made genuine contact with his own mind and consciousness before he dared shrink it into words.*[6]

CONTEMPLATION

The midrash teaches that when God gave the Torah and there was total silence, the sound came forth, "I am Hashem your God."[7] Rabbi Shimshon Pincus explains that it was not that everyone was quiet so they could hear the voice. Rather, the midrash is teaching us that when there is total silence, the preexisting truth comes forth...that Hashem is our God.[8] Sometimes, we have to close our ears to hear the truth.

Rabbeinu Bachya ibn Pakuda notes that most of the earlier *tzaddikim* (Hevel, the Avos, the twelve tribes, Moshe) were shepherds because of the benefits of solitude.[9] The benefit is more than hearing the truth of the world; it is also about hearing oneself. Research demonstrates that when people are alone, they are more likely to be creative and gain a deeper understanding of themselves and their priorities.[10] When we are alone, we are less concerned with how we appear to others. We can then focus more on how we appear to

---

6   Akiva Tatz, *The Thinking Jewish Teenager's Guide to Life* (Targum, 1999).
7   *Shemos Rabbah* 29:9.
8   Rabbi Shimshon Pincus, *Shabbas Malkesa*, Introduction.
9   *Shemos* 3:1.
10   Christopher R. Long and James R. Averill, "Solitude: An Exploration of Benefits of Being Alone," *Journal for the Theory of Social Behaviour* 33, no. 1 (2003): 21–44.

ourselves. When one is with oneself, it's easier to be one's self. It's then easier to know one's self.

Many have lost the value in contemplation. Rarely will you hear a politician in a public debate respond, "That's a good question...let me think about that for a moment." Thinking before answering is unfortunately perceived as a weakness—in direct contrast to the statement in *Avos* that the wise person does not immediately respond.[11] When somebody would ask Rabbi Shlomo Wolbe a question, he rarely answered immediately. He would almost always pause—sometimes for a minute or two—even when he knew the answer.[12]

Brief moments of thinking make a tremendous impact. Many patients and supervisees remark that the most powerful and insightful moments occur during the mindfulness exercises, in the moments of silence.

Insight occurs in the space between the words.

Rabbi Moshe Shapiro was giving a lecture and one of the students set up a tape recorder that paused when there was silence. When Rabbi Moshe noticed this, he said that the pauses are there for a purpose—the pauses allow for the teachings to be internalized. They are Torah too.

Emotion penetrates between the words.

Rabbi Ahron Soloveitchik explained that *Az Yashir* is written with spaces because it is a song. A song expresses emotion. Pausing allows us to fully experience the emotion and for it to affect us.[13] As the midrash states: The Torah was given as white fire inscribed with black.[14]

----

11   *Avos* 5:7.
12   Heard from Rabbi Wolbe's *talmid,* Rabbi Benzion Bamberger.
13   Heard from his grandson, Rabbi Shmuel Marcus.
14   *Midrash Tanchuma, Bereishis* 1; *Yerushalmi, Shekalim* 6:1 (25b). In *Menachos* 29a, it

The white fire, the space between the words, is just as important as the words themselves.

T R Y :

1. Try to do a mindfulness exercise with your eyes open. Notice how even in a relatively quiet room, there are so many noises. Notice the different sounds. Next, try to be more aware of the noises of the mind. Notice what your mind is saying. Spend a few moments looking around the room. Notice the different features in your environment that you weren't previously paying attention to.

2. When you are in a conversation with another or a group of people, instead of focusing on what you can share, try to listen to what others are saying. Insight and wisdom are more likely to be obtained in listening than in talking.

---

states that every letter in the Torah must be surrounded by parchment. The space is essential.

CHAPTER 18

Authenticity and Wholeness

Peace is when each one knows his place
and tries to fulfill his own purpose.[1]

Maharal

My eighth-grade *rebbi* had a sign hanging in the front of the room that read, "Be Real ~~Cool~~." At that age, the emphasis was on letting go of the cool. As we grow older, the challenge shifts to focusing on how to be real. Being real includes being aware and honest with ourselves. It even includes admitting when we are trying too hard to be real.

KNOWING YOUR SELF

Earlier, we discussed the metaphor of a limousine driver who can mistakenly over-identify himself with the vehicle and forget who he really is. He can mistakenly take pride or shame in the vehicle while forgetting that he is merely the driver. Still, to properly drive the limousine he has to know what it is capable of. Accordingly, although

---

1   *Derech Chaim* 1:18.

we should be careful not to take too much credit for the qualities God endowed us with, we must still be aware of them and use them. God gave us all different traits—some that may appear to be strengths and some that may appear to be weaknesses. We are charged with using our entire self to serve Him.

Looking into ourselves and clarifying our personal inclinations will help us find our path. "Just as people's faces differ one from another, so do their points of view."[2] We are all created differently and are meant to serve differently. God does not need me to be you, and you do not need to be me. We each have a personal mission to fulfill.

In the prayer on Yom Kippur we state: "My God, before I was created, I did not exist (*eini k'dai*) and now that I have been created, it is as if I was not created." Rabbi Kook explains this prayer as stating that before I was created, there was no need for me. The fact that my soul has now entered the world signifies that there is currently a purpose for me to fulfill. Now that I have been formed, I have a mission to accomplish. Unfortunately, we can fail to fulfill our role. If so, it is as if I have not been formed.[3]

Only I can be I and only you can be you.

> *When Reb Noach, the son of Rabbi Mordechai of Lekhovitz, took over after his father's death, his disciples noticed that there were a number of ways in which he conducted himself differently from his father, and they asked him about this. "I*

---

2   *Berachos* 58a.

3   *Olat Re'iyah*, vol. 2. Heard from Rabbi Mayer Twersky, who said that Rabbi Soloveitchik would often quote this idea of Rabbi Kook. It is also found in Soloveitchik, *Out of the Whirlwind*, p. 149.

do just as my father did," he replied. "He did not imitate, and I do not imitate."[4]

One of the forty-eight ways to acquire Torah is *"ha'makir es mekomo*—recognizing one's place."[5] We are at our best when we are most honest with ourselves and aware of our strengths and weaknesses. Mindfulness can help us discover who we are. Pausing and reflecting on our thoughts and inclinations increases self-awareness.

When one of my daughters received an electric toy as a present, she was pressing all the different buttons and nothing was working. As her frustration grew, I went over to help. We read the instructions and slowly discovered how to operate the toy. It's often worth taking a few minutes to discover how something works before we try to make it work. In the haste to do, we miss things. Unfortunately, we can miss important things about ourselves. Slowing down and reflecting helps us recognize what is working and what is not. Knowing ourselves helps us better navigate the terrain of life.

EMBRACING OUR SHADOW SIDE

When incorporating mindfulness into psychotherapy, it is not just a form of treatment. It is also used for assessment. Mindfulness can help people become more aware of what's truly bothering them. Many don't pay enough attention to their mind to notice what's taking place there.

Sometimes, when we become more aware of our thoughts, we don't like what we see. The unpleasant thoughts and desires which we would prefer not to have are what Swiss psychiatrist Carl Jung described as the shadow within us. Denying the shadow side has

---

4   Buber, *Tales of Hasidim*, p. 157.
5   *Avos* 6:6.

consequences. Shlomo HaMelech writes: *"Baz l'davar yechavel lo"*[6]—When you belittle something and do not give it its recognition, it will cause you harm.[7] Not recognizing our animalistic nature prevents us from taking the necessary precautions to deal with it. The Torah was specifically given to man because he has a shadow side.[8] There is no need for dejection regarding our unpleasant thoughts and desires. In fact, the *Baal Hatanya* wrote that perhaps this very struggle itself is what we were created for.[9]

VALIDATING THE STRUGGLE

In addition to struggling with desire, humans struggle with other unpleasant emotions, such as sadness or anxiety. Nobody likes these feelings. However, in many cases, what compounds the unpleasantness of the feeling itself is the very struggle with the feeling. The very thought, "I shouldn't be sad right now," or, "What's wrong with me for feeling anxious?" makes us feel worse. Therefore, making peace with ourselves in the present moment requires us to reconsider what is the "normal" state. If our expectation is that we are constantly supposed to be feeling good, we will be disappointed when we are not in the blissful state we wished for. When we accept that it is OK for life to be challenging, we can more easily embrace the present moment and pursue what is important to us.

For myself, the following idea by Rabbi Soloveitchik is comforting, as it validates the struggle in the religious journey. He writes:

> *Religion is not, at the outset, a refuge of grace and mercy*
> *for the despondent and desperate, an enchanted stream for*

---

6   *Mishlei* 13:13.
7   This idea and the reference to Carl Jung is from Batya Gallant, *Stages of Spiritual Growth* (Devorah Publications, 2010).
8   See *Shabbos* 88b–89a.
9   *Tanya* 27.

crushed spirits, but a raging clamorous torrent of man's consciousness with all its crises, pangs, and torments. Yes, it is true that during the third Sabbath meal at dusk, as the day of rest declines and man's soul yearns for its Creator and is afraid to depart from that realm of holiness whose name is Sabbath, into the dark and frightening, secular workaday week, we sing the psalm, "The Lord is my shepherd; I shall not want. He maketh me to lie down in green pastures; He leadeth me beside the still waters" (Ps. 23), etc., etc., and we believe with our entire hearts in the words of the psalmist. However, this psalm only describes the ultimate destination of homo religiosis, not the path leading to that destination. For the path that eventually will lead to the "green pastures" and to the "still waters" is not the royal road, but a narrow, twisting footway that threads its course along the steep mountain slope, as the terrible abyss yawns at the traveler's feet.[10]

According to Rabbi Soloveitchik, it is OK to find the religious journey challenging. In fact, it is the challenging road itself that eventually leads to the "green pastures." Some may find difficulty with this idea by stating that Rabbi Moshe Feinstein attributed the large numbers of children leaving Judaism to hearing their parents say, "*S'iz shver tzu zain a Yid*—It is difficult to be a Jew." I agree—it is detrimental to constantly hear that it is difficult to be a Jew. Still, teaching that a Jewish life is full of constant bliss is incorrect.[11]

---

10   Soloveitchik, *Halakhic Man*, fn. 4.

11   When the *Rambam* (*Hilchos Dei'os* 6:7) describes how to properly admonish someone who sins, he says you should tell him that you are encouraging him to mend his ways for his benefit in the World to Come (he does not say that it will be better for him in this world). Similarly, the *Derashos HaRan* writes (*derash* 6) that Avraham's willingness to sacrifice Yitzchak was due to his belief in the next world.

A healthier message can be that a religious life may be challenging, yet beautiful—and overall leads to a happier life for most people. The most beautiful things in life are born out of pain. Living an authentic religious life contains struggles, but the pursuit of a meaningful life makes it worth it. To live as religious Jews, we may need to forgo certain pleasures, but it is for the sake of something much greater. Moreover, in pursuing our values, we are more likely to achieve a more enduring happiness—eudaemonic happiness—the happiness that comes from meaning.[12] Paradoxically, as we stop chasing happiness, we are more likely to find it.

PEACE AND WHOLENESS

When we look inward, we gain perspective on how different values pull us in different directions. For example, if my niece's wedding is in one city and my close friend's son is getting married the same night in a different city, I am conflicted. In choosing to attend my niece's wedding, I can reduce the guilt by rationalizing that my friend won't be too bothered by my absence, or by telling myself that we are not even such good friends. However, in doing so, I'm not only deceiving myself, but I am belittling the friendship. The more we care for something, the more it hurts when it cannot be fulfilled. When we are in such a situation, we can either stop caring, or we can learn to make space for the discomfort.

Facing the self includes facing such conflicts:

- There is a part of me that wants to enjoy the world more and there is a part of me that wants to separate myself from it.

---

12 The *Shulchan Aruch* writes (*Orach Chaim* 222:3): "A person is obligated to bless God for the bad with a whole mind and wanting soul in the same way that he would bless for the good, because for the servants of God, even the apparent bad can be their happiness and good. Since he accepted out of love what God decreed, he finds that by accepting this bad, he is serving God, which brings him happiness."

- There is a part of me that wants to have more time for self-care and there is a part of me that wants to spend more time helping others.

Facing the conflicts within can be painful. A world where things are black or white is so much simpler. But that's not the world we live in. Seeking truth requires facing the entire self and facing the struggle. Ironically, even as I write these words, I experience a sense of serenity. In admitting the warring nature within, the war temporarily stops. Observing the entire self with compassion—which is the essence of mindfulness—often brings peace.

According to Rebbe Nachman of Breslov, peace is the uniting of opposites.[13] It is the ability to reconcile differences. It is reconciling the differences between conflicting opinions and recognizing the differences within ourselves. Reconciliation is achieved either through compromise or synthesis. In compromise, each party has to give up something. Synthesis is the coexistence of seemingly contradictory ideas. The highest peace is the ability to make space for different ideas and for different emotions.

In Hebrew, the word *shalom*, peace, is related to the word *shalem*, whole. To be whole means that I am not fighting myself. I can hold the different parts of myself together. I can hold my different emotions in one large container. Rabbi Benzion Bamberger recalled that his *rebbi*, Rabbi Shlomo Wolbe, was once describing someone as an *adam shalem* (complete person). Upon inquiring what this means, Rabbi Wolbe replied with the following metaphor: If a person has a choice to say a blessing on a large, beautiful challah that is missing a piece or a small roll that is whole, the small whole roll is preferable. To be whole is not to dismiss parts of ourselves. Peace is achieved by making space for the entire self.[14]

---

13   *Likutei Moharan* 80.
14   See *Rashi, Berachos* 60b. Regarding the mandate to say a blessing for the bad in the same

T R Y :

1. Begin by sitting and noticing your breath. After a few moments, try to begin noticing the sounds in the room. Next, try to pay attention to your thoughts. Just notice where they're going. Notice what thoughts you have about your thoughts—notice if you have certain judgments about where your mind goes.

2. What parts of yourself are you not so happy with? See if you can just be aware of them and notice what your mind says about them. If discomfort shows up, see if you can make space for it. Just like we can hold a crying baby with compassion, we can hold our crying emotions with compassion.

3. Try to dedicate some time to evaluating your strengths and weaknesses. Notice what thoughts show up when considering these.

---

manner that we bless God for the good, *Rashi* states: "You should bless suffering with a whole heart." We should strive to be fully present in life—both the good and the bad. As we open up our hearts to the present moment, we can find the beauty underlying the pain.

CHAPTER 19

Faith and Humility

Your heart will become proud, and you
will forget Hashem, your God.

Devarim 8:14

Regarding the arrogant, God says, "He and
I cannot dwell together in the world."

Sotah 5a

I was recently practicing a mindfulness exercise, and upon becoming more aware of what was going through my mind, I noticed that it was bombarded with unpleasant thoughts about
everything not going the way I'd like it to. When that happens,
my immediate reaction is to go into fixing mode by trying to solve the
struggles. But there are many times when that doesn't work. Either I
can't solve it, or if I do solve it, another difficulty arises.

Therefore, I decided to let go for now (at least for a few hours).
Perhaps I don't need to fix everything around me. Perhaps I don't

even need to fix everything about myself today. I have to stop playing God, and let Him run the show. Recognizing God's sovereignty makes it easier to manage life's challenges. We don't have to fix everything ourselves.

In *The Spirituality of Imperfection*, the authors write:

> *The spirituality of imperfection begins with the recognition that trying to be perfect is the most tragic human mistake. In direct contradiction to the serpent's promise in Eden's garden, the book Alcoholics Anonymous suggests, "First of all, we had to quit playing God." According to the way of life that flows from this insight, it is only by ceasing to play God, by coming to terms with errors and shortcomings, and by accepting the inability to control every aspect of their lives that alcoholics (or any human being) can find the peace and serenity that alcohol or other drugs (money, material possessions, power, or privilege) promise but never deliver.*[1]

Faith entails letting go of our illusory reins. We have to put in effort, but perhaps not as much as we think. When practicing mindfulness, we are temporarily letting go from doing. For some, this can be difficult. They don't want to let go—even for a few moments. But it's OK. The world is not going to fall apart if we let go.

Letting go can be an act of faith—it is recognizing that God is in control. That's why Shabbos is not just about desisting from work to have more time to think about God. It is even more: the not doing itself teaches us God is in control and it reminds us of our dependence on Him.

---

1   Ernest Kurtz and Katherine Ketcham, *The Spirituality of Imperfection* (New York: Bantam, 1992), p. 5.

LIVING WITH DOUBT

The desire for control is not limited to the physical; it is also found in the intellectual realm. The pursuit of knowledge and certainty enhances the sense of control. We strive for certainty about the world, our life, and our future. There is a part of me that wants to have it all figured out—unfortunately, that's never going to happen. Or, fortunately that's never going to happen, because that's not what's intended. We live in an age when we can have immediate answers to almost every question. If you are unsure of the year George Washington became president, you can immediately turn to your phone and google the answer.[2] In our modern age, we may soon forget what it's like to stay with the question, to sit with doubt, to live with uncertainty.

LETTING GO

Even within religion itself, we can try to control too much. In Rabbi Soloveitchik's *Lonely Man of Faith*, he describes the two sides of man:

- Adam I strives to create and conquer.
- Adam II submits himself to God.

Adam I doesn't only try to conquer the physical realm, he also wants to conquer the spiritual realm. At times, it appears that many religious individuals tilt toward Adam I, who

> *attends lectures on religion and appreciates the ceremonial, yet he is searching not for a faith in all its singularity and otherness, but for religious culture. He seeks not the greatness found in sacrificial action but the convenience one discovers in a comfortable serene state of mind…His efforts are noble, yet he is not ready for a genuine faith experience which requires the giving of one's self unreservedly to God,*

---

2   He became president in 1789. (Thank you, Google!)

> *who demands unconditional commitment, sacrificial action, and retreat.*[3]

Faith requires letting go of even "conquering" in the spiritual realm. Although religion is ultimately for our benefit, it should not be treated as another self-help tool. Many have their own vision of how they think they can best serve God, but there are many times when God steers us in a different direction.

Genuine faith requires sacrifice. Faith requires the willingness to sacrifice control, honor, and even the "pursuit of spirituality." Spirituality can unfortunately become an unhealthy means of fulfilling selfish desires. We should ensure the journey to God is not derailed to a journey to some other end.

We can learn to do our best with that which is within our power and let go of that which is beyond us. We can learn to balance Adam I with Adam II. The balanced Jew recognizes his role as a faithful servant, fulfilling his duties, putting in appropriate effort, and simultaneously recognizing that God is in control. This dialectic is beautifully manifested in the following conversation from the Talmud:

> *The men of Alexandria asked Rabbi Yehoshua ben Chananyah, "What must one do to become rich?"*
>
> *He answered, "Engage in business and do it honestly."*
>
> *They responded, "But many have done so and it did not work."*
>
> *He replied, "Rather they must seek mercy from He who provides wealth."*[4]

---

3   *Lonely Man of Faith*, p. 103.
4   *Niddah* 70b.

The Talmud asks: If prayer is essential, then why do you need to work? Because each one on its own does not suffice. We need both. We need to put in effort and pray. We need to do our part and recognize that it is only a part.

FAITH IN PAIN

Mindfulness entails facing reality and not being overly consumed by the emotions in the moment. Sometimes, facing the present reality can be very painful. Maintaining faith in troubled times requires humility.[5] It requires recognizing that we are limited in control and limited in knowledge. We cannot fully understand God's ways. We cannot always understand why certain things happen.

In one of his lectures, British philosopher Alan Watts popularized the following parable of the Chinese farmer:

> Once upon a time, there was a Chinese farmer whose horse ran away. That evening, all of his neighbors came around to commiserate. They said, "We are so sorry to hear your horse has run away. This is most unfortunate." The farmer said, "Maybe."
>
> The next day the horse came back bringing seven wild horses with it, and in the evening, everybody came back and said, "Oh, isn't that lucky. What a great turn of events. You now have eight horses!" The farmer again said, "Maybe."
>
> The following day, his son tried to ride one of the horses, and while riding it, he was thrown and broke his leg. The neighbors then said, "Oh dear, that's too bad," and the farmer responded, "Maybe."

---

5   In addition to humility serving as a prerequisite for faith, faith increases humility. In Rabbi Avraham ben HaRambam's chapter on humility, he describes how becoming closer to the Divine increases man's recognition of his own limitations.

The next day, the conscription officers came around to conscript people into the army, and they rejected his son because he had a broken leg. Again, all the neighbors came around and said, "Isn't that great!" Again, he said, "Maybe."

Watts continued:

The whole process of nature is an integrated process of immense complexity, and it's really impossible to tell whether anything that happens in it is good or bad, because you never know what will be the consequence of the misfortune. Or you never know what will be the consequences of good fortune.

We have all experienced moments when we were distraught about something, but in the end, it turned out well, as well as times when exciting opportunities led to disappointment. But the emotions in the moment can prevent us from recognizing that there is a bigger picture. Still, letting go of what we think makes sense does not invalidate the immediate emotional reaction to pain. It is part of the human experience. It is expected that we will rejoice for the seemingly good and be frustrated with the apparently bad. For that reason, we have a different blessing for good news and bad news.[6] In this sense, the Jewish philosophy would be different from that of the Chinese farmer. We give greater credence to the immediate emotional experience while simultaneously believing that it is ultimately for the best.

---

6   The Talmud in *Berachos* 60b asks: If there is a separate blessing for each, then how do we understand the statement, "A person is obligated to bless for the bad just as he blesses for the good"? The Talmud answers that it is teaching us to accept both with *simchah*. Interestingly, *Rashi* does not translate *simchah* as happiness, rather, he says we should bless misfortune with a complete heart. We should be fully open to the experience.

As Rabbeinu Bachya ibn Pakuda writes in his chapter on reflection:

> *In reflecting on the affairs of the world, you should always look to the final outcome of things, whether they be misfortunes or opportunities. You will often discover that many things happen to us against our will and we applaud their end results. The reverse is also true.*[7]

Perhaps, instead of saying "maybe," we could say, "This is unfortunate. I should try to do what I can to fix it while recognizing that it is in God's hands. Eventually, I will understand the purpose of this event—either in this world or the next."

The following idea beautifully illustrates the balance of validating a painful experience while simultaneously realizing that it is ultimately for our best.

> *Rabbi Moshe of Kobryn would say, "When a person suffers, he shouldn't say, 'That's bad! That's bad!' Nothing that God imposes on man is bad. Rather, he should say, 'That's bitter!' For among medicines, there are some that are bitter."*[8]

Pain is bitter. But sometimes that which is bitter can be good for us, and that which is sweet can be harmful. Reminding ourselves that it is ultimately for our best can make the pain more manageable. We don't have to understand how the medication heals—we just need to trust the doctor. To trust the doctor, we have to admit that He knows more than we do.

This is manifest with Rabbi Akiva, who was accustomed to go through life saying, "All that God does is for the good."

---

7   *Chovos Halevavos*, "Reflection."

8   *Or Yesharim*, p. 57.

> *Rabbi Akiva was traveling by a certain city and nobody invited him into their homes. When this occurred, he said, "All that God does is for the good." When he went to sleep in the field that night, a wind extinguished his lantern, a cat ate his rooster, and a lion devoured his donkey. After each misfortune, Rabbi Akiva replied with equanimity, "All that God does is for the good." It was later discovered that an enemy army came and captured the city, and if it weren't for these apparent misfortunes, Rabbi Akiva could have been captured as well.*[9]

Rabbi Akiva saw individual events as part of a bigger picture and therefore took things lightly. He did not berate those who did not let him in, and he did not complain about losing his possessions. He recognized that our limited minds cannot comprehend what the consequence of any specific event will be. Sometimes, like Rabbi Akiva, we will be fortunate to see the positive outcome in this world. However, with some challenges, we will only understand the purpose of the pain and misfortune in the World to Come.[10] There are some questions to which we are not privy to the answers—at least not now. Faith takes over where logic cannot go. Faith requires letting go, stepping back, and making room for another. It requires the painful recognition that "I don't know." It requires humility.

T R Y :

1. Sit still and do nothing for five minutes. Notice what shows up for you. Notice if there is discomfort in the non-doing, in the letting go. Remind yourself who's really in control.

---

9   *Berachos* 60b.

10   See Chazon Ish, *Emunah U'Bitachon*; see also Daniel Stein, "The Limits of Religious Optimism: The Hazon Ish and the Alter of Novardok on Bitachon," *Tradition: A Journal of Orthodox Jewish Thought* 43, no. 2 (2010): 31–48.

2. Think of different events in your life where an initial worry turned out OK. As Mark Twain said, "I have spent most of my life worrying about things that have never happened."

3. Remember that God is always by our side. I'm often inspired how right after people lose someone close to them, they proceed to say, "May His Great Name be blessed for eternity." No matter what you're going through, God loves you—even if you cannot feel it. God is with us in our darkest times. As one patient said when going through a very difficult time, "God, I don't know why this is happening, but I'm not giving up. I'm not going to let this stop me from believing in You."

CHAPTER 20

Rabbi Akiva— A Mindful Model

We all need role models. Even if we are aware of our values, there is a benefit to finding a human being that encompasses such values. The benefits are twofold: (1) The role model serves as a source of inspiration, and (2) the role model helps concretize the values in a practical manner; the theory is put into practice.

This is why we connect to stories. A story delivers an experience; an experience delivers in a way that a didactic teaching cannot. It moves beyond the intellect. It fuses the mind with the heart. When our heart is touched, we are more likely to shift our behavior.[1] Therefore, there is a benefit in identifying a model of mindfulness. Although most of our great leaders throughout our history probably lived mindfully, for the purposes of the story, let us focus on the life

---

1   Paul J. Zak, "Why Inspiring Stories Make Us React: The Neuroscience of Narrative," In *Cerebrum: The Dana Forum on Brain Science*, vol. 2015 (Dana Foundation, 2015).

of the Tannaic Sage Rabbi Akiva. Let's reflect on the life of one of the greatest Jewish leaders as a role model of mindfulness.

THE LESSON OF THE ROCK

In *Avos D'Rebbi Nosson*, the following story is told:

> *What was the beginning of Rabbi Akiva? He was forty years old and had not learned a thing. One time, he was standing by a well and asked, "Who carved this rock?" He was told, "The water that consistently falls on it, day after day." Upon seeing his wonderment, they said, "Akiva, did you not read, 'Water wears away stones' (Iyov 14:19)?" Immediately, Rabbi Akiva concluded: "If water, which is soft, can carve a hole in a hard rock, then words of Torah, which are as hard as iron, can transform my heart, which is but flesh and blood!" Immediately, he returned to learn Torah.*[2]

When I look at a rock, I see a rock. Actually, I barely even see the rock; I am mostly in my mind—only somewhat noticing my environment.

When Rabbi Akiva saw the rock, he was not only in tune with his environment, but he saw so much more than the rock itself. He saw what it could teach him. He was able to learn from his environment.

For a long time, I misunderstood this story. I incorrectly interpreted the metaphor of the water and rock as teaching that if a person keeps on striving toward a specific goal, step by step, he can make a tremendous difference. Although this lesson is true, this is not how the metaphor was understood by Rabbi Akiva. In the metaphor, he is not the water, he is the rock. It was not the difference that he could make on the world; rather, it was what the Torah could do to him. Each drop of Torah makes an impact on someone in a way that

---

2   *Avos D'Rebbi Nosson* 6:2.

cannot be seen immediately. His primary goal was not how he could refine the world, it was how he could refine himself.

FOLLOWING YOUR VALUES

When Rabbi Akiva decided that he should begin to learn Torah, the midrash relates that he was concerned about the potential embarrassment of a forty-year-old sitting in a classroom among little children learning the *aleph-beis*.[3] With her profound psychological wisdom, his wife advised him to take a donkey, plant some vegetables on top of it, and take it to the marketplace. Initially, people mocked, but after a few days, they stopped.

From this incident, Rabbi Akiva learned that he could follow his values independent of what others are thinking. Perhaps he also recognized that he could move toward his values independent of what his own inner critic was saying. He did not let his critical mind and the accompanying emotions hold him back from continuing on his worthwhile path.

MEANING IN THE MOMENT

When I am disappointed with my lack of progress in certain areas, I console myself with the fact that Rabbi Akiva began his career at the age of forty. For many, Rabbi Akiva serves as the paradigm for achieving greatness despite starting at such a late age. However, I do not believe that Rabbi Akiva was striving for greatness in the intellectual sense. The ability to patiently go to school day after day for twenty-four years does not stem from a potential hope to be a great scholar; he had no way of knowing that he would eventually be the leader of the generation. Rabbi Akiva found meaning in what he did day by day. He found meaning in learning the *aleph-beis* because that itself was his way to serve God. His success came because he learned Torah like an ox serves its master (see chapter 15, "Mindfulness and

---

3   *Midrash Hagadol, Shemos* 4:13.

Talmud Torah"). He recognized the value in the process, not just the destination.

BEGINNING AGAIN

After twenty-four years, Rabbi Akiva's greatness was known, and he was a teacher of twenty-four thousand students. Unfortunately, a great tragedy occurred and all of his students died.[4] Rabbi Akiva did not let the past hold him back from moving forward. He knew what it meant to live with a beginner's mind. He began anew, teaching five new students who would continue the tradition. He experienced emotion, but was not held back by emotion. He did not let his pain deter him from moving forward. Rabbi Akiva was able to start afresh with each breath of life.

THE TREES AND THE FOREST

While living in the present, Rabbi Akiva simultaneously saw beyond the present. When Rabbi Akiva and three other Sages were walking by the place where the Holy Temple had stood and saw a fox leave from the location of the Holy of Holies, three of the Sages were crying and Rabbi Akiva was laughing. When the Sages asked him why he was laughing, he replied that seeing the fox was a fulfillment of the prophecy of destruction, and just like the prophecy of destruction was fulfilled, so too the prophecy of redemption will be fulfilled.[5] Rabbi Akiva saw the present moment in the context of a greater history.

There are a series of experiments demonstrating that emotions in the present moment influence our overall description of life. For example, minor events such as finding a dime or the outcome of a sports game may influence how one rates their life as a whole.[6] It

---

4   *Yevamos* 62b.
5   *Makkos* 24b.
6   Norbert Schwarz and Fritz Strack, *Well-being: The Foundations of Hedonic Psychology*

is the nature of man to magnify what he is thinking about in that moment. Rabbi Akiva was able rise above this. He did not let specific events alter his perception of reality. He was able to view the present moment in the context of an overall life of serving God. He was able to see the trees and the forest.

ANCHORED IN MEANING

Rabbi Akiva did not get tossed by the vacillations of life; he was anchored in what he needed to do in the present. He was anchored with meaning. Upon surviving a shipwreck, Rabbi Gamliel asked Rabbi Akiva how he survived. He replied, "I held onto this plank of the ship and every time a wave came, I moved my head from there."[7] The manner in which he survived the sea was the way he traveled through life; he held onto that which was important and did not get pulled by the waves.

Life brings a variety of waves. The Talmud recounts that four Sages, Ben Azai, Ben Zoma, Acher, and Rabbi Akiva, entered the *pardes*.[8] Though the literal translation of *pardes* is orchard, *Rashi* states that they entered the Heavens using the Divine name. The Talmud describes that Ben Azai died from the experience, Ben Zoma lost his mind, and Acher became a heretic. Only Rabbi Akiva emerged safely. The *Maharsha* explains that Rabbi Akiva survived because he was cognizant of the limits of the human mind. While others may have been pulled by the lure of spiritual heights, Rabbi Akiva knew where to stop. He didn't get pulled by the waves of spirituality. Sometimes, the greatest self-control is putting the brakes on spiritual strivings.[9]

---

7 (Russel Sage Foundation, 1999), "Reports of Subjective Well-Being: Judgmental Processes and Their Methodological Implications," pp. 61–84.

7   *Yevamos* 121a.

8   *Chagigah* 14b.

9   This is consistent with Rabbi Akiva's statement that *Shir Hashirim* is the holiest of holies

GOD IS ONE

For Rabbi Akiva, the natural culmination of a life dedicated to serving God was dying for the sake of God.[10] When the Romans charged Rabbi Akiva with teaching Torah, they sentenced him to death and tortured him slowly with an iron comb. With each brush, he reaffirmed his faith in God. When his students asked, "Does one have to go this far?" Rabbi Akiva replied that throughout his life he was concerned that he may not be able to fulfill the verse, "With all your soul," which teaches us that we have to be willing to give up our life for God. In his last moments, he was finally able to fulfill this. As he neared physical death, he prayed: "*Shema Yisrael, Hashem Elokeinu, Hashem Echad,*" and his soul departed with *Echad*.[11]

How does one give up his *nefesh*, his very being? It must be that there is more to one's being than the physical body. Our truest identity is not our body, it is the *neshamah*. This is the part that nobody can reach, nobody can take from us. In that moment, Rabbi Akiva connected to his truest self. He utilized his free choice to rise above nature. He held onto the plank and was not swayed by the waves.

(*Yadayim* 3:5). Only the Kohen Gadol on Yom Kippur can enter the Holy of Holies. Rabbi Akiva knew that certain places are not to be entered (heard from Rabbi Eytan Feiner).

10   This idea is adapted from Rabbi Mayer Twerksy's *hesped* for his brother, Rabbi Moshe Twersky, Hy"d.

11   *Yerushalmi, Berachos* 9:5.

Conclusion

A   s I traveled on the journey of writing this book, I ended up in places I did not expect. At the outset, I intended to gather information and sources on mindfulness, yet as I continued, I gained a greater appreciation for the value of inner wisdom. I tried to slowly place more trust in myself. Wisdom is more than a collection of aphorisms. It includes looking into oneself and learning from oneself. Life is our greatest teacher; this moment is the greatest teacher. If we fully open our eyes, ears, and emotions, we will tap into its profound wisdom. We are all students, but we are also all teachers. We can learn from the world and ourselves. Everyone has something to contribute.

In my early years working as a clinical psychologist, if I had a few extra minutes before the next patient was arriving, I would pull a relevant book from the shelf to see if there was any new information I could use to help the patient. Although there was a benefit to this, I now believe I can be more helpful if I use the time to be mindful of inner wisdom and reflect on what the patient needs in the moment. When stuck, the immediate reaction is to seek external solutions, but if we slow down and reflect, we will find that many answers can be found within. We just need to pay attention.

In the beginning of life, the physical trajectory is upward; every day we are becoming bigger, smarter, and stronger.[1] Subconsciously, this creates an illusion of immortality, for although the sixteen-year-old intellectually knows that he will not live forever, his everyday experience tells him otherwise. At a certain point, the trajectory is no longer upward; we begin to notice that our body cannot accomplish what it used to. Experience eventually meets the intellect in facing mortality. As I write this, I find myself at such a point. I can no longer fool myself saying I am going to work on this tomorrow, for today is yesterday's tomorrow.

We are only in this world for a limited amount of time. Don't wait to ask, "What do I truly want to accomplish?" "How do I want to live?"

Hillel writes: "If I am not for myself, who will be for me?"[2] If I don't accomplish what is expected for me, nobody else can. I am the only one that can be me. There are certain tasks in this world that only I can fulfill. This need not be something objectively grand. I am my child's only father; I am my wife's only husband. Only I can fulfill those roles.

Hillel continues: "If I am for myself, what am I?" As I fulfill my purpose, I should continue to ask, "What am I?" Pausing, reflecting, and questioning is a lifelong process. I must also remember my true identity. I am a *neshamah*; I am part of something greater than myself.

Hillel concludes: "And if not now, then when?" If I am not present, then what do I really have? If I am not paying attention to what's happening to me in this moment, then when I am going to truly live?

Let us begin the journey.

---

1   Part of this paragraph is based on a *shiur* from Rabbi Mayer Twersky.
2   *Avos* 1:14.

About the Author

Jonathan (Yoni) Feiner, PhD, is the clinical director of Rockland CBT, a psychology practice group specializing in mood and anxiety disorders. In addition to his work as a clinical psychologist, he has taught courses and provided workshops on topics related to Judaism, psychology, and mindfulness, in academic and community settings.

Prior to receiving his PhD from Hofstra University, Dr. Feiner studied in Yeshivat Kerem B'Yavneh and in Yeshiva University's Rabbi Isaac Elchanan Theological Seminary (RIETS). He lives with his wife and children in New Hempstead, New York. He welcomes any questions or feedback to his email: RocklandCBT@gmail.com.

וזכני לגדל בנים ובני בנים חכמים ונבונים אוהבי ה'
יראי אלקים אנשי אמת זרע קדש בה' דבקים ומאירים
את העולם בתורה ובמעשים טובים ובכל מלאכת
עבודת הבורא.

Dedicated to the loving memory of

יעקב בן אהרן אריה ז"ל

רבקה לאה בת עזריאל ז"ל

JACOB AND LILY FEINER, ז"ל

יוסף משה רפאל בן צבי הירש ז"ל

עדינה בת אליעזר ז"ל

JOSEPH AND ADINA RUSSAK, ז"ל

Leonard and Bobbee Feiner
and family